Ha Ha Ha! Ha Ha Ha! Ha Ha Ha!

Laugh Scotland!

Laugh Scotland!

Allan Morrison

www.vitalspark.co.uk

The Vital Spark
is an imprint of
Neil Wilson Publishing Ltd
Suite Ex 8, Pentagon Centre
44 Washington Street,
GLASGOW
G3 8AZ

Tel: 0141-221-1117
Fax: 0141-221-5363
E-mail: info@nwp.co.uk
www.vitalspark.co.uk
www.nwp.co.uk

A catalogue record for this book is
available from the British Library.

ISBN 978-1-903328-41-7
Typeset in Bodoni
Designed by Mark Blackadder
Printed in Poland

Ha Ha Ha! Ha Ha Ha! Ha Ha Ha! Ha Ha Ha!

Ha Ha Ha!
Ha Ha Ha!
Ha Ha Ha!
Ha Ha Ha!
Ha Ha Ha!
Ha Ha Ha!
Ha Ha Ha!
Ha Ha Ha!
Ha Ha Ha!
Ha Ha Ha!
Ha Ha Ha!
Ha Ha Ha!

Ha Ha Ha!
Ha Ha Ha!
Ha Ha Ha!
Ha Ha Ha!
Ha Ha Ha!
Ha Ha Ha!
Ha Ha Ha!
Ha Ha Ha!
Ha Ha Ha!
Ha Ha Ha!
Ha Ha Ha!
Ha Ha Ha!

Contents

Introduction

IT IS SAID that all Scots love jokes and have a great sense of humour ... perhaps because it's a free gift! However, humour can be very personal, so there is plenty in this book to choose from. *Laugh Scotland!*, the all-Scottish jokes book, is designed to make you and your friends smile, and spread some fun around oor wee country and beyond.

The Scots are a proud and idiosyncratic race. This is probably due to our history, our geographic position ... but mainly the weather. As a result our jokes tend to be robust and irreverent, no doubt caused by our well-developed, often dry, sense of pungent wit. We abhor pretension but seem to delight in our self-deprecating ways.

Unfortunately thrift, prudence and dourness have come to be regarded as distinct Scottish characteristics. Nothing could be further from the truth. Although we do have a strongly developed sense of independence, the Scots are generally a hospitable, gregarious, noisy, and generous race. We love nothing better than fun and a wee joke.

Telling a joke properly requires a little practice. You need to go over all aspects of the story in your mind before you launch forward. Remember, to tell a good joke well, set the scene clearly. This is crucial. Assume your audience has never heard the joke ... a proper lady or gentleman should never admit to having heard it before or, worse still, steal your punch-line. Tell it simply, with no coughing or giggling. Scots people like their jokes straight. Don't embroider it too much, judge the mood of the listeners and deliver the correct punch-line. Screwing up the ending will be your ruin! And never laugh at your own joke ... until the audience do.

If you can tell a good joke well, then you're an okay sort of person. Anyone can do it with some patience; and the ability to tell a joke is deemed to be a useful social skill, like dancing or playing card games.

Where do Scottish jokes come from? Nobody knows, but they certainly don't come from south of the border!

Jokes are good for your health. In fact, it is said laughter is a tranquilliser with no side effects.

So, laugh and live long and well.

Go ahead and read this book – enjoy! Gie yersel' a guid laugh!

Glasgow
and
Edinburgh

Q. What's the difference between Edinburgh and Glasgow?
A. Breeding. In Edinburgh breeding is very important – in Glasgow, it's fun!

Ha Ha Ha!

Two Glasgow women were talking. 'Of course the good thing about having a Marks and Spencer in Glasgow is that you can buy yer knickers there and change them in Edinburgh.'

Ha Ha Ha!

A woman from Morningside was out driving when a car ran into her. The following day a policeman came round to her house to take some details.

'Now, madam. Can I ask you what gear you were in?'

'Well, officer. It was a red Windsmoor jacket, with black Jaeger trousers from Harvey Nichols.'

Ha Ha Ha!

A man in Glasgow was caught shoplifting in Argos. He had stolen a brochure and two pens.

Ha Ha Ha!

The American President was making a visit to Scotland. For weeks the American Secret Service and the CIA had been checking out a posh Glasgow golf course where the President and the Scottish First Minister would play. No one was allowed to play or be near the course for the week leading up to the event.

On the day, as the two VIPS and their security men stopped to take their approach shots to the third green, two wee Glasgow boys came out of the bushes and offered to sell them lost golf balls.

Ha Ha Ha!

Q. What's the difference between Edinburgh Zoo and Glasgow Zoo?
A. Edinburgh Zoo has a description of the animal in front of the cage. Glasgow Zoo has the recipe.

Ha Ha Ha!

Glaswegians consider Edinburgh to be in the east – The Far East.

Edinburgh folk consider Glasgow to be in the west – The Wild West!

Ha Ha Ha!

An Edinburgh chap met an old acquaintance, Jimmy, from Glasgow. Jimmy rudely pointed to the pot belly that the Edinburgh fellow had developed over the years, and asked, 'What are you going to call it?'

'Well, if it's a boy I'll call it Donald after Scotland's original First Minister. If it's a girl I'll call it Elizabeth after our most gracious Queen. But if it's only wind, I'll call it Jimmy!'

Ha Ha Ha!

Q. What's the difference between the Edinburgh Mafia and the Glasgow Mafia?

A. The Edinburgh Mafia make you an offer you can't refuse. The Glasgow Mafia make you an offer you can't understand!

Ha Ha Ha!

A Glaswegian staying in a hotel in Edinburgh phoned Room Service for some pepper.

'Would that be white pepper or black pepper, sir?'

'Naw. Toilet pepper!'

Ha Ha Ha!

A visitor to Edinburgh was walking along Princes Street, when a fierce dog appeared and attacked a small boy. Disregarding his own safety, the man grabbed the dog and throttled it to death.

A reporter from the *Edinburgh Evening Gazette* arrived on the scene and shook the hero by the hand. Then he informed him that the headline in the newspaper would read, 'Brave Local Hero Saves Child by Killing Vicious Beast!'

'But I'm not from Edinburgh,' protested the man.

'Okay, in that case we will run a headline that says, "Kind Stranger to Edinburgh saves Child by Killing Dog".'

'But I'm not really a stranger to Edinburgh. I'm from Glasgow!'

That night the headline read: 'Glaswegian Slays Family Pet!'

Ha Ha Ha!

A Glasgow man who was married to an Edinburgh woman came home one morning off the nightshift and went straight up to the bedroom. He found that his wife had the blankets pulled over her and was snoring. Needing his conjugal rights, he crawled under the blanket and proceeded to make love to her. Afterwards he decided to go downstairs for something to eat but was startled to find his wife in the kitchen making coffee.

'How did you get downstairs without me seeing you after we made love?' he asked his wife.

'Oh, no!' exclaimed his wife, 'that's my mother up there. She came on the train from Edinburgh last night, complained of a headache, and I told her to lie down.'

Rushing upstairs, the wife ran into the bedroom. 'Mother, I cannot believe this has happened. Why didn't you say something?'

The mother-in-law huffed and said, 'I haven't spoken to that good-for-nothing Glaswegian for ten years and I wasn't about to start now!'

Ha Ha Ha!

Q. What do you call an Edinburgh man who's lost 75 per cent of his intelligence?
A. Divorced!

Ha Ha Ha!

Q. How many Glasgow men does it take to change a toilet roll?
A. Who knows, it's never happened!

Ha Ha Ha!

Ha Ha Ha! Ha Ha Ha! Ha Ha Ha! Ha Ha Ha!

Puzzled doctor to patient in a Glasgow Medical Centre.

'Huv ye had this before, Mrs McClinty?'

'Yes, doctor.'

'Aye, weel ye've goat it again!'

Ha Ha Ha!

'What are you doing lying in the gutter?' asked the Glasgow policeman. 'Are you drunk?'

'Aye, pissed oot ma mind!'

'What are you doing lying in the gutter?' asked the Edinburgh policeman. 'Are you drunk?'

'No. I've just found this parking space, so I've sent the wife off to buy a car!'

Ha Ha Ha!

A man in Glasgow bought a bed. It came in two halves that had to be assembled at home.

When he drove up to his house, he left one half of the bed in his estate car while he took the other part inside. When he came out the second half had disappeared.

He immediately went round to the local police station. There were two queues at the enquiry desk; one for the public and the other for a group of prostitutes waiting to be charged.

The man finally got to the top of the public queue, and explained the situation to the desk sergeant. 'Well, sur,' said the policeman, 'we might just be able to solve your problem right here and now.'

He turned and shouted to the prostitutes: 'Hey! Ony o' youse part-time?'

Ha Ha Ha!

Passers-by were amazed to see a builder walking nonchalantly along the steel beams high above the half-finished Scottish Parliament in Edinburgh. When the worker came down someone said to him. 'That was fantastic to see you walking across these beams without a safety harness or a net underneath. How did you do it?'

Said the steel erector, 'It's really no problem. I used to drive a school bus in Glasgow until my nerves gave out!'

Ha Ha Ha!

The guide was explaining to the group of locals some facts about Edinburgh Castle. 'This part of the castle,' he explained. 'has not been altered or replaced in any way for over eight hundred years.'

One woman turned round and whispered to another, 'See that Edinburgh Council!'

Ha Ha Ha!

A guy went up to a woman in an Edinburgh nightclub and asked, 'How do you like your eggs in the morning, darling?'

She blushed and said, 'Well done.'

The following evening the same chap went up to a woman in a Glasgow nightclub and asked, 'How do you like your eggs in the morning, darling?'

'Unfertilised!'

Ha Ha Ha!

Both cities are environmentally friendly. Edinburgh folk drive unleaded cars. Glasgow folk go to unleaded churches.

Ha Ha Ha!

A Glasgow motorist broke down as he drove through Edinburgh. He flagged down another car and asked the driver to give him a hand.

'I'm sorry,' laughed the other motorist, 'but I'm a chiropodist.'

'Ok, pal,' replied the Glaswegan, 'in that case could you gie's a tow!'

Ha Ha Ha!

The Glasgow motorist was in court. He had decided to challenge his speeding fine.

'And what makes you so sure you were only doing ten miles an hour?' asked the JP.

'Ah wis goin' tae the dentist!'

Ha Ha Ha!

Some Glasgow women can be very naive. They think that mutual orgasm is an insurance company in Edinburgh!

Ha Ha Ha!

The customs officer opened the suitcase of an Edinburgh woman just off a flight from Scotland. There he found six pairs of very small pants. Taking them out for further inspection, he noticed that they were all labelled with one day of the week, from Monday to Saturday.

'And on Sunday?' he enquired.

She blushed and said, 'Just the fur coat on Sundays.'

The next person to be inspected off the flight was a rather large woman from Glasgow. The customs officer pulled out 12 pairs of massive knickers. Before he could say anything, the woman smiled and said, 'January, February, March, April ...'

Ha Ha Ha!

A waiter in an Indian restaurant in Edinburgh, asked the diner, 'Curry okay, sir?'

'Yes, lovely thank you, waiter.'

A waiter in an Indian restaurant in Glasgow, asked the diner. 'Curry okay, sir?'

'Naw, ah cannae sing a note!'

Ha Ha Ha!

Glasgow folks are always ready to stop and lend a hand.

A motorcyclist gave his friend a lift and as the friend did not have any leathers to keep out the cold, suggested that the individual should put his coat on back to front.

The motorcyclist decided to show his friend just how fast the motorbike could go and fairly sped around George Square. Suddenly he hit a bump and, looking round, saw he had lost his passenger. Someway back he spied a crowd of people looking down at a prone figure on the road, and he turned around and rode back. 'Is he all right?' he anxiously asked one of the group.

'Well,' came the reply, 'he wis until somebuddy turned his head roon!'

Ha Ha Ha!

The Edinburgh policeman waved down a motorist. 'When I saw you coming along the road there, madam, I just thought – 50 at least.'

The woman quickly replied, 'Well, you see officer, I always look older in this black hat!'

Ha Ha Ha!

The wee Glasgow boy and the wee Edinburgh lad were paddling in the sea at Rothesay.

'My goodness,' exclaimed the Edinburgh lad, 'your feet are very dirty!'

'Aye, we didnae come last year.'

Ha Ha Ha!

Q. What is the most common proposal of marriage in Edinburgh?
A. Darling, I love you dearly. Will you marry me?'
Q. What is the most common proposal of marriage in Glasgow?
A. Ye're whit?

Ha Ha Ha!

An Edinburgh chap came across a motorist with the bonnet of his car up.

'What's the matter?' asked the good citizen.

'Oh, the piston has broken,' replied the motorist.

'In that case, I recommend you call the RAC.'

A Glasgow fellow came across the same motorist with the bonnet of his car up.

'What's the matter?' asked the Glaswegian.

'Och, piston broke.'

'Me tae, pal!'

Ha Ha Ha!

An Edinburgh chap came home early of an afternoon, only to find his wife busily trying to cover up the obvious signs of wild sex.

'Was it my friend Alexander?' he yelled.

'No, it wasn't,' she replied.

'Well, was it my friend Robert?' he demanded.

'No, it certainly was not,' she answered. 'Anyway, don't you think I have friends of my own?'

Ha Ha Ha!

The funeral of the old Glaswegian was in progress. The minister was talking about the old man's life, what a model of the community he had been, a loving father, a loving husband, and how he had never tasted whisky in his life. At that the widow could stand it no more. She said to her son, 'Listen, Jimmy, jist you go up there an' have a wee look in that coffin. Ah think we're at the wrang funeral!'

Ha Ha Ha!

A wee boy had fallen on the pavement in Edinburgh. When he got up he staggered a bit and shook his head.

'Have you got vertigo?' asked a passer-by.

'No, I was just clearing my head. I'm fine now, thanks.'

A wee boy had fallen on the pavement in Glasgow.
When he got up he staggered a bit and shook his head.
'Have you got vertigo?' asked a passer-by.
'Naw mussis. Jist roon the corner.'

Ha Ha Ha!

Scotsmen

The 65-year-old Scottish millionaire married a 19-year-old beauty queen.

'Ye old devil!' exclaimed his friend. 'How did ye manage it?'

'Ah told her ah wis 95!'

Ha Ha Ha!

'Ma great grandfether had the second sight, ye know,' exclaimed Hamish to his pal. 'He even knew the exact year and month he wis gonnae die. In fact, he even knew the date and time of day.'

'That's jist uncanny,' said the pal. 'Did he ever say how he knew all this?'

'The judge told him.'

Ha Ha Ha!

Two Scotsmen were drifting in a lifeboat on the ocean. Their ship had sunk many weeks before and they were getting desperate. Suddenly they saw a bottle bobbing about on the waves. They opened the bottle and out popped a genie. 'Sorry,' said the genie, 'but I have been trapped in that bottle for many years and my powers have waned. I can only give you one wish.'

Impulsively one of the men shouted out. 'I wish the ocean was all whisky.'

Immediately the men found themselves floating on a sea of the finest malt.

'Ya eejit!' yelled the other Scot. 'Noo we're gonnae have tae pee in the boat!'

Ha Ha Ha!

A man opened his front door and there stood his mother-in-law. 'Nice to see you, mother-in-law. It's been a long time since you were here. Do come in. How long will ye be staying for?'

'Just until you get tired of me,' she replied.

'Whit, are you not even going tae stay for a wee dram!'

Ha Ha Ha!

Two old men were sitting on a park bench in Falkirk. One said to the other, 'You know, Wullie, we've been sitting here so long that ma bum has fallen asleep.'

'Ah know,' said the other one, 'ah heard it snoring!'

Ha Ha Ha!

An old farmer came into town on market day and took the opportunity to visit his doctor.

'I wid be very grateful, dochtor, if the next time you are oot near the farm you could call in and see the wife.'

'No problem,' replied the doctor. 'Is your dear wife ill?'

'I dinnae ken, doctor,' said the farmer. 'But jist yesterday morn she got oot the bed at the usual time o' four o'clock, milked the coos and made the breakfast fur me and the lads. Then she did the farm accounts, made the lunch, churned the milk, fed the chickens, ploughed a couple o' fields before making the dinner. Then she went and painted the inside o' the barn. But the thing is ... aboot ten o'clock she complained aboot being a wee bitty tired. If you ask me, doctor, ah think she needs a wee tonic or something.'

Ha Ha Ha!

The Scot went to the chemist. 'Dae ye hiv ony poison tae kill mice?'

'Sorry, sir. Have you tried Boots?'

'Dinnae be daft. Ah want tae poison them, no' kick them tae death!'

Ha Ha Ha!

Two Scots were staggering home one star-filled night after spending some hours in the pub.

'Is that the sun or a moon up there?' asked one.

'Ah widnae know,' replied the other, 'ah'm no' fae aroon these parts.'

Ha Ha Ha!

A drunk gets on a bus late one night, staggers up the aisle and sits next to a woman. She looks him up and down, sees the bottle in his hand, and says, 'I've got news for you. You're going to hell!'

'Oh, naw! Ah've goat oan the wrang bus!'

Ha Ha Ha!

Three old Scots farmers were sitting having their dram in the pub, discussing their various aches and pains. The 70-year-old said, 'I have this problem in the mornings. When I get up at seven o'clock, it takes me aboot 15 minutes tae pee!'

The 75-year-old said, 'Och, ma problem is worse. I get up at eight o'clock, an it takes me 15 minutes tae pee, then anither half hour tae grunt an' groan tae have a crap.'

'Well,' said the 85-year-old farmer, 'At seven I pee like a pig, and at eight I crap like a coo.'

'So, what's your problem?' asked the other two.

'Ah, dinnae wake up till nine!'

Ha Ha Ha!

A women answered her door to a charity worker who said: 'Hello there, I'm collecting for the home for drunks. Could you contribute something, please?'

'Certainly, dear,' said the woman, 'jist hold on a minute till he puts on his jacket.'

Ha Ha Ha!

Two men were walking towards each other on King Street, Aberdeen. Both were dragging their left leg as they walked. As they met, one looked at the other knowingly and said, 'Falklands War, some years back.'

The other one pointed behind and said, 'Dog dirt, 20 yards back.'

Ha Ha Ha!

Willie and Jimmy were sentenced to be shot by a firing squad.

'Do you have any last requests?' asked the officer.

'Aye,' replied Willie, 'I want tae listen to a Sidney Devine record afore I go.'

'And what about you?' the officer asked Jimmy.

'Shoot me first!'

Ha Ha Ha!

A woman was walking near the Waterfront in Greenock when she saw a man with a peg-leg, a patch over one eye and a hook in place of a hand. 'Wow,' she thought, 'a real life pirate!' So she went up to him and asked how he had lost his leg?

'Well,' he said, 'I was going to Rothesay on the paddle-steamer, Waverley, when I leaned over the rails to see the paddles turning, toppled over, and lost ma leg.'

'Oh, dear,' she exclaimed, 'and how about your hook?'

'Well,' he said, 'I was in the butchers and I pointed to a leg of ham I wanted sliced and, quick as a flash, I lost ma hand in the slicer.'

'Oh, dear, dear,' she exclaimed, 'and what about the patch?'

'Well,' he said, 'I was walking along, not far from this very spot, when a seagull did its business right in ma eye.'

'But how could that make you lose your eye?' she asked.

'It wis the first day ah had oan the hook!'

Ha Ha Ha!

A drunk was duly brought before the court in Inverness. Just before proceedings could begin there was a bit of a commotion in the public gallery.

'Order, order!' shouted the Sheriff.

The drunk said, 'Thanks, pal. Ah'll have a double malt and a beer chaser.'

Ha Ha Ha!

A Glasgow drunk decides to pop into the cinema. He buys his ticket and staggers in, staggers out a minute later and buys another ticket, then staggers in again. A minute later goes out to buy another ticket.

'Do you realise, mister,' said the girl in the ticket office, 'you've bought three tickets.'

'Ah know,' replied the drunk, 'but every time ah go in a wee wuman tears it in half!'

Ha Ha Ha!

A Scot goes into a pub and says to the barman. 'I'll have a wee celebration drink. Gie's a double and have one for yourself.'

'So what's the big occasion?' asks the barman.

'Ma wife has just run aff wi' ma best friend.'

'My goodness! But why are you no' sad?'

'Sad!' exclaimed the Scot. 'They've saved me a fortune! They're baith pregnant!'

Ha Ha Ha!

The tourist came whizzing round a bend on a Highland road and ran over a dog. A distraught farmer's wife ran over to the dead animal.

'I'm very sorry, madam,' said the tourist. 'Of course I'll replace him.'

'Ah'm no' so sure about that,' she replies. 'How are ye at rounding up sheep?'

Ha Ha Ha!

Q. What's the difference between a Scottish funeral and a Scottish wedding?

A. There's one less drunk at the funeral!

Ha Ha Ha!

Sandy and Willie were out walking when a heavy shower of rain started.

'Quick, Sandy,' said Willie, 'put your umbrella up or we'll get soaked.'

'I cannae, Willie. It's got holes in it.'

'Holes in it? Why on earth did you bring it?'

'I didnae think it would rain!'

Ha Ha Ha!

A man put his hand out of his tenement window to see if it was raining. Just as he did this a glass eye fell into his hand. Looking up he saw a young woman looking down from the window of the flat above.

'Is this yours?' he asked.

'Aye, could you bring it up, please?'

When he got to the flat he saw that she was a most attractive lady. She offered him a dram, and then invited him to bed.

As he was leaving he asked, 'Dae you act like this with every man you meet?'

'Naw,' she replied. 'Jist them that catch ma eye.'

Ha Ha Ha!

The drunk is staggering along Argyle Street in Glasgow, asking various people the time. 'Ah don't understaun,' he moans, 'ah've asked six folk the time an' ah get a different answer every time.'

Ha Ha Ha!

A Dundee man won a toilet brush as the booby prize in a raffle. A few weeks later a friend asked him if he was getting much use out of his toilet brush.

'Well,' came the reply, 'Ah dinnae think much o' it. In fact ah'm thinkin' o' goin' back tae using toilet paper.'

Ha Ha Ha!

A Glasgow man went into marriage with both eyes closed. His wife's brother closed one and her father closed the other.

Ha Ha Ha!

Q. How do most Scotsmen define marriage?
A. A very expensive way to get their washing done.

Ha Ha Ha!

A Scot and his wee boy were standing in front of the lion enclosure at Edinburgh Zoo. The father was explaining that the lion was a ferocious beast who was king of the jungle. 'Dad,' said the wee boy, 'see if one of these lions escaped just now and ate you up …'

'Yes, son,' said his father expectantly.

'What's the number of the bus I should get home?'

Ha Ha Ha!

When an optimist sees a half empty glass he says it's half full.

When a pessimist sees a half empty glass he says it's half empty.

When a Scotsman sees a glass half empty he says, 'Hey, barman!'

Ha Ha Ha!

One night, at about midnight, a worried Perth woman phoned her vet to ask what she should do about her dog and bitch who were romantically entwined in the living-room.

'Why don't you tell them they're wanted on the phone?' he suggested.

'My goodness! And will that work?' she exclaimed.

'Well, it worked for me!'

Ha Ha Ha!

A Scot went to the doctor. 'Jist look at this, doctor,' he said, 'ah cannae get ma hauns tae stop shaking.'

'Do you drink much whisky?' asked the doctor.

'No' any more. Ah spill most o' it!'

Ha Ha Ha!

An Edinburgh couple went to the zoo. Unfortunately a lion dragged the woman into its den. The animal keeper appeared, and seeing the woman and the lion facing one another, said. 'I'd better go and get my rifle.'

'Don't be daft,' replied the husband, 'the lion got itself into this mess.'

Ha Ha Ha!

A tourist was going for a stroll through a small Highland village. She couldn't help but notice a wrinkled old man with a white beard sitting outside a cottage, with a huge, happy smile on his face.

'Excuse me, sir, I hope you won't take offence, but you look so content. What is your secret for such a long life?'

He replied, 'I drink two bottles of the finest malt whisky every day, smoke 80 fags each day, never eat fruit or vegetables and never exercise.'

'Amazing,' exclaimed the tourist, 'and how old are you?'

'Twenty-two.'

Ha Ha Ha!

A newspaper seller was standing at Central Station in Glasgow. 'Read all about it,' he shouted. 'A hundred Scots swindled! A hundred Scots swindled!'

Curious, a passenger bought the paper and checked the first six pages. Finding nothing, he complained to the newspaper seller. 'Hey, there's nothing in here about a hundred Scots being swindled.'

The newspaper seller completely ignored him and went on shouting. 'Read all about it! One hundred and one Scots swindled!'

Ha Ha Ha!

The Clydeside shipyard trade union steward was feeding back to his members about how his negotiations with management had gone. 'Wages are doubled, backdated from six months ago, holidays are increased to three months a year, and we only have to work on Mondays.'

A man at the back shouted, 'Whit! Every Monday?'

Ha Ha Ha!

Do you think that Moses led the Israelites through the desert for 40 years because God was testing him, or because he wanted them to appreciate the Promised Land when they got there?

No, it's because Moses was a Scotsman ... and refused to ask anybody for directions!

Ha Ha Ha!

A police car suddenly stopped outside the Morningside bungalow. Old Fred was helped into the house by a young officer, who explained to Fred's wife that the elderly gentleman had been found lost in the local park.

When the police had gone, Fred's wife said. 'Lost in the park? You've been going there every day for the last 15 years.'

'I wasn't lost. I was just feeling too tired to walk home!'

Ha Ha Ha!

A Scotsman died and was standing in line at the Pearly gates waiting to be judged. Away to his right he could see Satan throwing poor souls into a fiery pit. Occasionally Satan would stop and put a soul on a small pile by his side.

The Scotsman's curiosity got the better of him and he walked over to the Prince of Darkness. 'Excuse me,

Jimmy, [he came from Glasgow] but why are you tossing aside some souls instead of flinging them into the fire?'

'Well, ye see,' replied Satan. 'They're from Greenock and they're too wet to burn.'

Ha Ha Ha!

A man went into a Glasgow police station. He asked the officer at the desk, 'Are there any criminal lawyers in Glasgow?'

'Aye, sur,' replied the sergeant, 'but we cannae prove it!'

Ha Ha Ha!

The Scot was in the pub, obviously down at the mouth.

'Ma Uncle Jimmy wis ma best pal,' he informed the barman. 'See when ah wis a wee boy he took me everywhere, taught me tae swim, bought me ma first bike, took me tae aw the matches. An' noo ah huvnae seen him for over ten years,' he sighed, 'an' ah feel that guilty.'

'Has he passed away?'

'Naw, he's won the bloody lottery!'

Ha Ha Ha!

The two pals were climbing up Ben Nevis when one of them lost his footing and fell down a ravine 500 feet deep.

'Are you okay, Archie?' called the man at the top.

'I'm just about alive, Bobbie,' came the reply.

'Here, grab the rope,' shouted Bobbie, throwing down a rope to Archie.

'I cannae haud it,' replied Archie. 'baith ma arms are broken.'

'Well, twist it roon yer legs.'

'I cannae dae that either, Bobbie. Baith legs are broken tae.'

'Well, put the rope in you mooth,' shouted Bobbie. So Archie managed to bite on the rope and Bobbie began to slowly haul him to safety – 400 feet … 300 feet … 200 feet … 100 feet … 25 feet … And then Bobbie shouts, 'Still okay, Archie?'

'Aye e e e e e e e …'

Ha Ha Ha!

A Glasgow thief had just been released from Barlinnie Jail and was out celebrating on the town with his girl-friend. Just as they passed a jeweller's she saw a large diamond ring in the window. 'Hey, ah wish ah'd that ring,' she exclaimed.

'Nae problem,' said the boyfriend, throwing a brick through the window and grabbing the ring.

A couple of streets further on his girlfriend stopped to admire a leather coat in a shop window. 'Whit ah wid give tae own that!' she exclaimed.

'Watch this, hen,' said the boyfriend hurtling a brick through the window and snatching the coat.

Ten minutes later they came to a garage selling lovely, shining Jaguars. 'Ah'd dae anything fur wan o' them,' she said coyly to the boyfriend.

'Fur heaven's sake,' he moaned, 'dae ye think ah'm made o' bricks!'

Ha Ha Ha!

A man was mugged by a fearsome individual in Aberdeen. He had no cash on him so, fearing violence, offered to write the mugger out a cheque.

The mugger was astonished. 'A cheque! Why would ah take a cheque fae you. I dinnae even ken ye!'

Ha Ha Ha!

Jimmy went to the airport to pick up his friend Gordon. When he got there he found Gordon in tears. 'Ah lost the best part o' ma luggage on the way here,' he moaned.

'Do you think it was stolen?'

'Naw, the cork came oot!'

Ha Ha Ha!

An Edinburgh man was approached by a stranger in the street, 'I'm doing a project on self-defence. Would you know how to defend yourself against a karate attack?'

'Sorry, no. I'm afraid I wouldn't.'

'Great! Gie's yer wallet and watch!'

Ha Ha Ha!

The young man was clearly nervous. 'Mister MacIntosh, I wish to marry your daughter.'

'And are ye sure ye can support a family?' asked the father.

'Well, I've done ma sums, Mister MacIntosh, and I'm pretty certain I can.'

'But dae ye realise there are ten o' us?'

Ha Ha Ha!

School pals, Willie and Archie, had left school about 20 years previously and in all that time they had not met. Then there was a class reunion and they met again.

'So how has life been treating you, Archie, since we left school?'

'I've had my ups and downs but generally it's been quite good. I'm now the Chairman of a large bank, and my wife and I have homes in Scotland, England, New York and the French Riviera. What about you, Willie?'

'Well, I must say that life has been tough. I married that wee cracker, Allison Forsyth, you know the blonde that sat just in front of us in class. Within six months she had run off with another man. Then to make matters worse my next wife ran off too ... with a woman! The house I had in St Andrews burned down and I'd somehow forgotten to renew its insurance. Then I was stuck by a golf ball on the course and was in a coma for over a year. Recently I was run over by a bus and now have an artificial leg. And on the way to this reunion tonight I was mugged.'

'If you don't mind me asking,' said Archie, 'what do you do for a living?'

'Ah sell lucky white heather!'

Ha Ha Ha!

Two Scots were having a late night drinking session. The discussion got round to the weight of babies in the days of rationing just after the war.

'When ah wis born, ah wis only twa pounds.'

'Jings! An did ye live?'

'Did ah live? Ye ought tae see me noo!'

Ha Ha Ha!

A Motherwell man took his dog to the vet and asked that the dog's tail be removed.

The vet said, 'Well, we can do it if you want but your dog has such a long bushy tail it does seem a shame. Why do you want it done?'

'Ma mither-in-law is comin' tae stay an' ah don't want the least wee bit sign of welcome!'

Ha Ha Ha!

'Hello, hello! Is that Kilmarnock police station?' came the anxious voice.

'Yes, sir, it is.'

'Do you have any reports of lunatics escaping near here, officer?'

'Not that I know of, sir. Why are you asking?'

'Someone's run off wi ma wife!'

Ha Ha Ha!

At the Highland town fete, Auld Hamish won virtually every prize. He won prizes for tomatoes, carrots, potatoes, neeps and peas. As the Provost presented Auld Hamish with his awards, he asked him what was the secret of his success. 'Och, it's easy,' commented Auld Hamish. 'It's manure, manure and even more manure.'

The Provost's wife was listening to the conversation and turning to Auld Hamish's wife commented, 'It's a pity your husband keeps on talking about manure all the time. It sounds awful, putting such a thing on those vegetables. Could he perhaps not use another word?'

'Listen, dearie, its taken me 40 years tae get him tae say, manure!'

Ha Ha Ha!

A drunk walks into a pub in Dundee and shouts, 'Barman, a round for the house, and have one yourself!' The crowd in the pub cheer, the barman takes all the orders, passes round the drinks, then knocks one back himself.

'That'll be £95 for the round,' says the barman, to which the drunk replies, 'I'm stony broke.'

The barman is furious. He drags the man to the door and throws him into the street.

The next night, the same drunk walks in again and says, 'Barman, a round for the house, and have one for yourself, too!' The crowd cheer and the barman decides that nobody would come into the pub and do the same thing twice. He thinks that he might also pay for the previous night's round too. So he passes round the drink and knocks one back himself.

'OK, that's £95 for last night, and £105 for tonight,' he says, to which the man replies, 'Sorry, pal, but I'm still skint.'

The barman, goes wild, punches the man and throws him out the pub onto the street.

The following night, the barman is amazed to see the same fellow come in and shout, 'Barman, a round for the house.'

'What!' says the barman, 'nothing for me this time?'

'No fear,' says the guy, 'one drink and you get really nasty!'

Ha Ha Ha!

A Highlander died and went to heaven. At his audience with the Almighty he said, 'O Lord, I just want to thank you for my long life in the most beautiful country in the world, with its sparkling lochs, mountains, salmon, oil, and of course, the whisky. And as an appreciation of my gratitude I've brought you a bottle of the finest malt.'

'How thoughtful of you,' replied the Almighty. 'Is there anything else you wish to say?'

'Aye, that'll be 25 pounds!'

Ha Ha Ha!

Three elderly Scots were discussing death and how they would like to leave this life.

'I would like to die,' said the first Scot, 'on my 85th birthday, immediately after I've climbed Ben Nevis and stuck a flag on the top.'

Said the second Scot, 'I'd like to die at 90, immediately after creating a new course record at St. Andrews.'

'I would like to die in bed at 100, once I've received ma telegram from the Palace,' said the third Scot, 'shot in the back by a jealous husband!'

Ha Ha Ha!

An armless man walked into a Scottish village pub. He ordered a pint and when it was served, he asked the barman if he could get the money out of his trouser pockets. The barman duly did this.

The armless man then asked the barman if he could lift the pint to his lips so he could drink it.

The barman duly did this.

He then asked the barman if he would get his hanky out of his pocket to wipe the froth from around his lips.

This the barman duly did.

He then asked the barman where the gents toilet was.

'Aboot five miles doon the road, pal,' came the reply.

Ha Ha Ha!

A Japanese soldier is found on a wee Pacific Island, many years after the end of World War Two. He is flown back to Tokyo to be reunited with his wife. After bowing low to greet her, he says, 'Very honourable wife, I have heard you have been living with a soldier from a place called Glasgow, in far off Scotland. Is this true and have you been faithful to me?'

'Michty me. Surely ye dinnae believe aw they filthy lies, Jimmy!'

Ha Ha Ha!

A Scotsman returned to London after a fishing holiday in Scotland. He was telling the other people in his office about the size of a fish he almost caught. 'I'll bet it was almost as big as the Loch Ness Monster,' jeered one of his colleagues.

'Loch Ness Monster,' said the man, 'I was using it for bait!'

Ha Ha Ha!

The man fell headlong down the Waverley Steps. As he picked himself up at the bottom, an old woman approached him. 'Did ye miss a step, son?'

'No, I hit every one of them!'

Ha Ha Ha!

A woman had been working in the finance sector in Edinburgh for years and the stress and strain had got to her. So she resigned from her job and bought a wee croft in a remote Highland glen in the middle of nowhere.

For over three months she did not see anyone, until one evening she heard a knock at the door. Standing there was a huge Highlander, resplendent in beard and kilt. 'Hello, my name is Donald. I'm your nearest neighbour. I'm from the next glen. I'm having a grand party on Saturday night and wondered if you would like to come along?'

'That's most thoughtful of you,' replied the woman, 'after over three months without human company I would just love to come.'

'Grand,' said Donald, 'but I had better jist warn you that there's gonnae be some serious drinking at this party.'

'Listen,' replied the woman, 'after working in Edinburgh for years I can hold my liquor with the best of them.'

'More then likely,' said Donald, 'there may be a wee bit fighting. It happens at these events, you know.'

'Listen I tend to get on with most people, so that shouldn't be a problem.'

'One final thing,' said Donald, 'you get some wild sex at these parties too.'

'I'm sure I'll be okay,' said the woman, 'what time should I come over?'

'Oh, any time you like.' replied Donald, 'There'll just be the two of us!'

Ha Ha Ha!

A Highland farmer knocked on the door of his neighbour's farm, and the neighbour's daughter answered the door. 'Is yer fether in?'

'No,' replied the girl. 'He's at the market in Inverness. If it's the services of the Aberdeen Angus bull ye want, the cost is £750.'

'No, no,' replied the farmer rather impatiently.

'Well,' said the daughter. 'If it's the Galloway bull you want, then it's £500.'

'No,' replied the farmer, 'it's not that either.'

'Well,' said the young girl, 'the Red Ayrshire Bull is just £200.'

'That's not what I'm here for whatsoever, lassie. Your brother Hamish has got my daughter pregnant. My wife and I want to know what your father proposes to do about it.'

'Well,' said the young girl, 'you'll just have to see my father yourself. I'm not so sure what he charges for Hamish.'

Ha Ha Ha!

A rambler went into a hostelry in the Highlands.

'Sorry, sir, the bar won't be open for an hour yet. Would you be wantin' a wee dram while you're waiting?'

Ha Ha Ha!

A father who worked offshore was home for two weeks out of every four. Each Saturday during his time at home he liked to take his children out for a ride in the car. Unfortunately, one Saturday he was in bed with the flu, and his wife, knowing that the children liked their little run in the car, opted to take the children herself.

When they got back to the house, the father asked his little boy if he had enjoyed the run in the car with mummy. 'Oh, yes, Daddy,' he replied. 'But do you know we didn't see one single bastard!'

Ha Ha Ha!

A wee Hamilton boy came home after a visit to Edinburgh zoo with his Dad.

'So, how was it, Ronald?' asked his mother.

'Oh, it was smashing. And Dad loved it too, especially when one of the animals came racing home at 20 to one.'

Ha Ha Ha!

A Scotsman drinks a glass of whisky every night. After years of this habit his wife decides that he should stop drinking.

One night she gets two glasses, puts whisky in one and water in the other. She puts them on the coffee table, then gets him to fetch his fishing bait. 'Now you watch this,' she says, and puts a worm in the glass of water where it swims around. She then takes the worm out and puts it in the whisky where it quickly expires. 'So,' she says, 'what do you have to say about that?'

'Well,' he says, 'if you drink whisky you won't get worms.'

Ha Ha Ha!

A Scottish Dad came home one day and told his six children that he had a surprise gift for them. 'Now,' he said, 'I've got a box of chocolates and I'm going to give them to the person who never answers Mummy back, and who always does what they're told. So, who's the winner?'

'You are, Dad!'

Ha Ha Ha!

On a very hot summer's day, a man decided to sunbathe nude in his back garden, which was surrounded by a huge fence.

'Ah wonder,' he said to his wife, 'whit the neighbours would say if they could see me?'

'They'd probably say I must have married you fur yer money!'

Ha Ha Ha!

A woman reported her husband's disappearance to the police. The officer taking all the details asked if there was any message they could pass on if they found him?'

'Aye,' said the woman, 'tell him ma mither didnae come efter aw!'

Ha Ha Ha!

An American, an Englishman and a Scot were talking over a drink in a pub. Soon they got on to describing their lives at home.

'Last night I made love to ma dear little, ole wife, three times,' the American bragged. 'And this morning she told me how much she loved me.'

'Well, chaps,' said the Englishman, 'last night I made love to my darling wife six times, and this morning she said that I was the most wonderful gentleman in the world.'

'And what about you?' the Englishman smugly asked the Scot. 'How many times did you make love to your wife last night?'

'Jist the wance!'

'Only once?' laughed the American, 'and what did she say this morning?'

'Don't stop, Jimmy!'

Ha Ha Ha!

The old Scots couple were driving south on the M6. They stopped at a service station for lunch. Unfortunately the old lady left her glasses on the table, but didn't realise this until they were some way down the motorway. Eventually they were able to find a flyover and turn round. The old man did nothing but moan and groan at his wife all the way back to the service station. When they got back, the old woman got out of the car to go in and try to find her glasses. The old man called after her, 'Mary, see when ye're in there, ye might as well pick up ma bunnet as well.'

Ha Ha Ha!

'I'm sorry to hear your marriage is o'er,' said Andrew. 'If you don't mind me asking, why did it break up?'

'Och, it was due to sea-sickness,' replied Donald.

'I didnae know your wife had been on a ship,' replied Andrew.

'She hadnae. She said she wis jist sick o' seeing me!'

Ha Ha Ha!

A wife was sick of her husband taking her for granted:

'Look at that Willie Jamieson across the road. Every morning when he goes to work he kisses her goodbye at the door. Why don't you do that?'

'But ah don't even know the wumin!'

Ha Ha Ha!

There was a display of wedding gifts some days before a wedding. Among the many lovely gifts was a large envelope from the groom's father, on which was written, 'Cheque for five thousand pounds.'

'Who is that strange man pointing at your father's cheque and laughing?' the bride asked the groom.

'That's ma fether's bank manager!'

Ha Ha Ha!

Scotswomen

'And how many children do you have, Mrs MacDougal?' asked the social worker.

'Four.'

'And what are their names?'

'Eenie, Meenie, Manie and Jimmy.'

'Thank you, Mrs MacDougal,' replied the Social worker. 'As a matter of interest, why did you call the fourth one Jimmy?'

'Because ah didnae want ony Mo'!'

Ha Ha Ha!

A woman in Perth went to see her solicitor to ask about a divorce.

'What grounds do you have?' asked the lawyer.

'Just a wee garden at the back,' replied the women.

'I don't think you understand. Let me rephrase my question. Do you have a grudge?'

'No, we park in the street.'

'Let me try again. Does your husband beat you up?'

'No, I'm always up at least half-an-hour before him.'

'Oh, for heaven's sake, madam. Do you really want a divorce?'

'It's not me that wants a divorce,' she replied. 'It's him! He says we can't communicate.'

Ha Ha Ha!

Women in Scotland think a transvestite is a man who changes his semmit every night.

Ha Ha Ha!

Two Scotswomen were talking. 'Surely you don't believe that story about your husband being out all night fishing. Ah mean tae say, he didn't even bring ony fish back.'

'That's why ah believe him!'

Ha Ha Ha!

Two Morningside ladies were having coffee in a fashionable Edinburgh café.

'My husband has just lost all his money and life savings in a stupid business venture. He's totally bankrupt. Not a penny in the world!'

'How dreadful, my dear,' observed the other lady, 'you must feel really worried about him.'

'I certainly am,' replied the other. 'I don't know what he's going to do without me.'

Ha Ha Ha!

The wee boy was playing on the sand at North Berwick. 'Can I go in the sea, Mummy?' he asked.

'Certainly not, Brian. Perhaps tomorrow. The sea today is very rough and dangerous.'

'But Mummy, Daddy is in the sea swimming.'

'I know, dear, but he's got plenty of Life Insurance.'

Ha Ha Ha!

Two Edinburgh ladies were talking. 'Would it kill you if your husband ran off with another woman?'

'Well, it might,' replied the other. 'They say that sudden, intense delight can cause heart attacks!'

Ha Ha Ha!

'Listen, Hamish, I had better warn you, my husband will be home in an hour.'

'But Stella,' protested Hamish, 'ah haven't done anything ah shouldn't do.'

'I know, but if you're going to, you'd better get a move on!'

Ha Ha Ha!

Two ladies in Glasgow were talking. 'You know I'm so, so worried. In fact I've lost ten pounds in weight since I found my husband's secretary's pants in the back of his car.'

'You should leave him and take that swine for everything he's got,' replied the other.

'Oh, don't you worry, I'm going to. First, though, I want to get down to nine stone!'

Ha Ha Ha!

'My wife is a very astute woman,' observed Wullie.

'How dae ye make that out?' asked his pal, Jimmy.

'Well, ye know how there have been a lot of burglaries in oor street, and we're in the Neighbourhood Watch Scheme. She's discovered a way of protecting aw they expensive clothes she bought. Every now and then when ah come in fae ma work, ah find the man from next door in the wardrobe guarding them!'

Ha Ha Ha!

A lady went into a clothes shop in Glasgow. 'May I try on the dress in the window?' she asked.

'Sorry, mussis,' came the reply, 'ye'll jist need tae use the changing-rooms like aw the other customers.'

Ha Ha Ha!

A middle-aged woman goes to see a fortune-teller in Airdrie.

'The future is wonderful for you,' said the fortune-teller. 'You will meet a rich, tall, dark, handsome stranger who will make you very happy.'

'Smashing!' exclaimed the woman, 'but whit dae ah dae wi ma husband?'

Ha Ha Ha!

An older woman was doing her morning exercises in front of the mirror. As she did so she was clearly admiring her figure.

'Whit are you looking at?' asked her husband.

'Well, my aerobics instructor says I have the legs of a 20 year old.'

'Aye,' observed her husband, 'but whit did he say aboot yer auld bum?'

'He never mentioned you!'

Ha Ha Ha!

'I've broken up with my fiancé.' The woman told her friend.

'How dreadful for you,' said her friend

'Aye, you're right,' said the woman, 'so I've just done the proper Scottish thing. I've sent him back his letter, all his Valentine cards and his wee presents to me.'

'Whit aboot the engagement ring?'

'Naw, ah'm holding on tae that fur sentimental reasons!'

Ha Ha Ha!

'Mummy, do all fairy tales begin with 'Once upon a time'?'

'No, ma wee pet. Some begin with "I had to stay late at the office, darling".'

Ha Ha Ha!

It was a warm day and the lady in a West Highland hostelry asked the waitress for something, long, icy and half-full of whisky.

'How about ma man, dear?' came the reply.

Ha Ha Ha!

A man had been ill for some time, and he and his wife went off to the seaside for a fortnight's holiday. The weather was wonderful, but, sadly just a couple of days after his return the man suddenly passed away.

As was the custom, prior to the funeral, the body was left at home for friends and relatives to pay their respects.

A neighbour came in to pass on her condolences, looked down at the prone figure and said to the widow. 'My, doesn't he look just grand. Ye can see that holiday in Rothesay did him the world o' good.'

Ha Ha Ha!

Two Edinburgh ladies were talking. 'Listen,' said one, 'Myra told me that you told her the secret I told you not to tell her.'

'Och, no,' said the other, 'I told her not to tell you that I told her.'

'Well,' replied the first lady, 'I told her I wouldn't tell you she told me what I told you not to tell her!'

Ha Ha Ha!

'Dearest,' said Sylvia to her husband Tom. 'every day you come home from the office in town, and I make a point of asking you how your day was. I sit and listen to all your tales of what happened during the day. I have your dinner all ready for you, your slippers and your *Herald* at the side of your chair. You know, you never ask me how my day was.

'Sorry,' said Tom. 'How was your day, darling?'

'Bloody awful! Don't ask.'

Ha Ha Ha!

Two Scots ladies were standing in the Crematorium. 'Ye know, ah blame masell fur Wullie's death.'

'How's that?' asked her friend.

'Ah shot the pig!'

Ha Ha Ha!

'Sandy thought of everything before he died,' Mary told her friends. 'On his deathbed he handed me three envelopes. "Mary," he said, "Ah've pit ma last three wishes in they envelopes. After I'm deed open them and do exactly as I have asked. Then I'll rest in peace."'

'What were in the envelopes?' her friends asked.

'Well, the first one contained two thousand pounds for a nice mahogany coffin. So I bought a lovely one for him.'

'The second envelope had five thousand pounds for the wake. Plenty of food and drink for his friends.'

'And what about the third one?' asked her friends.

'It had ten thousand pounds in it for a nice stone.'

Holding her hand in the air Mary said, 'Dae ye like it? It's ten carats!'

Ha Ha Ha!

'Where are you going on holiday this year?' a man asked his friend. 'Is it back to Millport?'

'Naw, it's a change this year,' he replied. 'We're going to Africa.'

'Are you no' worried the hot weather might disagree wi' your wife?'

'It widnae dare!'

Ha Ha Ha!

The handsome young man asked his Scottish girlfriend to marry him, pointing out that his father had a large Highland estate, was a multimillionaire, and was 105 years old.

The young girl asked her boyfriend to give her a little time to consider. Two weeks later she became his stepmother!

Ha Ha Ha!

A Scottish woman weighing 20 stone had a heart attack, and whilst in hospital had a out-of-the-body experience. Suddenly God appeared.

'Is that ma time up?' she asked him.

'Naw, hen,' (He is, of course, Scottish!) He replied, 'you've goat another 50 years tae go.'

When she was released from hospital she was determined to get fit. She attended Scottish Slimmers and got herself down to nine stones. She went to yoga classes and jogged 10 miles every day.

One day while she was out jogging, she was hit by a lorry and killed instantly. Standing before God she demanded, 'Hey. Ah though you said ah had 50 years tae go.'

God replied, 'Ah'm awfa sorry, hen, but ah didnae recognise ye!'

Ha Ha Ha!

Two women were talking about one of the men in their firm.

'See that Walter Kinloch,' said one, 'have nothing tae dae wi' him. He knows nothing but filthy songs.'

'Well, I've never heard him sing a dirty song in all the time I've been here,' said the other.

'Maybe not, but he certainly whistles them!'

Ha Ha Ha!

Two women were talking in Princes Street.

'Oh, hello, Mabel, and how is John?'

'Oh, did you not hear? John passed away a couple of weeks ago.'

'I'm dreadfully sorry to hear that, Mabel, and how did it happen?'

'Well, my dear,' explained Mabel, 'he had just gone into the garden to pull a lettuce for lunch when he collapsed with a heart attack.'

'How dreadful for you. So what did you do?'

'Oh, I just opened a wee tin of peas.'

Ha Ha Ha!

Suzanne was on the phone. 'May I speak to someone in the Mail Order department?'

'Speaking, madam.'

'Well, I'd like to order one. Scottish, about 35 to 40, fairly tall, reasonably well off, and kind to children and animals!'

Ha Ha Ha!

A new carpet in the family home was ruined when a tin of paint was knocked over onto it. The Glasgow wife phoned the insurance company and asked for money.

'I'm sorry, madam,' explained the insurance clerk, 'but insurance doesn't quite work like that. We ascertain the worth of the article, then provide you with a replacement of comparable value.'

'In that case ye can just cancel the policy on ma husband!'

Ha Ha Ha!

A couple were celebrating their silver wedding anniversary. 'You know, hen, there's something that's always worried me. Oot o' aw oor ten weans, wee Sammy looks different fae the rest. Ye wid think he had a different fether.'

'He has,' came the reply.

'Okay, ah can take it. Who is wee Sammy's fether?'

'You!'

Ha Ha Ha!

Q. What do you call a Scots woman with one leg?

A. Eileen.

Ha Ha Ha!

'My wife and I had a wee row on Friday night,' explained a Perth man to his pal. 'She wanted to go to the pictures and I wanted to go to the theatre.'

'And was the film any good?'

Ha Ha Ha!

The East Kilbride man was angry when he found out his wife had been cheating on him. He shouted at her, 'Dae ye think I'm gonnae play second fiddle tae this man?'

'Second fiddle! Ah'll huv ye know ye're lucky tae still be in the band!'

Ha Ha Ha!

'Will the father be present during the birth?' asked the nurse.

'Naw,' replied the mother-to-be. 'He an' ma husband never get on.'

Ha Ha Ha!

A woman in Edinburgh asked her husband if he could fix her vacuum cleaner that had broken down

'Definitely not! Dae ye think ma name's Hoover?'

The next day the washing machine broke down and she asked it he would repair that.

'Definitely not! Dae ye think ma name's Zanussi?'

The following day the TV broke down and she asked him to repair it.

'Definitely not! Dae ye think ma name's Sony?'

A few days later the husband came home and said, 'I see you got everything fixed. How did ye manage it?'

'It wis easy. Duncan from next door said he would fix them if I either slept with him or sang an auld Scots song.'

'So whit did ye sing?'

'Dae ye think ma name's Moira Anderson?'

Ha Ha Ha!

Jaimie said to his wife, Jean. 'Listen, hen, why don't we go out tonight and have some fun?'

'Great idea,' replied Jean. 'And if you get home afore me make sure ye leave the lobby light on.'

Ha Ha Ha!

A census clerk was slowly making his way around the flats in a Glasgow tenement. He eventually got to the top flat that an elderly lady occupied. She freely gave him various details, but when he asked her for her age, she refused to tell him.

'But everyone has to give me their age,' he protested.

'Well, did that auld pair o' spinsters doon the stair, Maggie and Jeannie Hill, tell you theirs?'

'They certainly did!' he informed her.

'Well, ah'm the same age as them, so there!' and she shut the door on him.

A few weeks later a print-out of everyone's information was sent out for verification. When the old lady opened hers, against her age it read: 'As old as the Hills.'

Ha Ha Ha!

A teacher from a High School in Ayr was an after-dinner speaker at a conference in Largs.

'As you know,' he began, 'I come from Ayr and I wish to frame my speech around these three letters.'

'A stands for Academia, something that all Scots should aspire to …' And he talked about Academia for 20 minutes.

'Y is for Youth, our future in Scotland …' and he went on about Youth for 25 minutes.

'R is for Receptive, we must ensure that our young people are receptive to education …' and he went on about being receptive for half-an-hour.

When he sat down he asked the Chairman, whose eyes had somewhat glazed over, how he thought it had gone.

'We enjoyed it very much,' said the Chairman, 'And we're awfa glad we asked you and not that other chap fae Campbeltown!'

Ha Ha Ha!

Scotsman to wife. 'Do you think, my wee pet, that in my next life I might come back as a worm?'

'Don't be daft, Donald. Sure ye always come back as something else!'

Ha Ha Ha!

The Scottish Parliament

The lads in an unfashionable part of a Scottish town were discussing the forthcoming elections for the Scottish parliament. The SNP had a candidate, Labour had a candidate and the Liberals had a candidate. But as yet there was no Tory.

'Ah'm gonny nominate wee Rab tae be the Tory candidate. He'd be jist rare.'

'Jist rare? An' whit's wee Rab goat that we huvnae goat?'

'Easy. He's the only wan in the district wi a suit!'

Ha Ha Ha!

An MSP was arrested for drunk driving. Asked to explain himself at the trial, he drew himself up, and began, 'Well, you see. I'm an MSP and ...'

'One thousand pounds and six points on your licence. Ignorance is no excuse!'

Ha Ha Ha!

The Scottish Parliament recently passed a bill to purchase new fire engines for all major Scottish towns and cities. The question was then asked as to what would happen to the old fire engines.

By 125 votes to 3 it was decided to keep them for false alarms.

Ha Ha Ha!

A man took his wee boy to see the opening of the Scottish Parliament. 'Daddy, why did that minister pray for all the MSPs?'

'No, no, son' replied the father. 'He wasn't praying for the MSPs. He was praying for the Country!'

Ha Ha Ha!

A chap went into an Edinburgh antique shop. A little brass mouse figure caught his eye and he asked the owner how much it was. 'It's 25 pounds plus a hundred for the story that goes with it.'

'It's okay,' said the chap, 'I'll just take the mouse.'

Examining it outside the shop, he noticed that the figure was actually hollow with small holes in the side. Holding it up to his mouth he blew into it and a strange, melodious whistle was heard. No sooner had he started walking when he noticed half-a-dozen mice following him. He continued to walk, every so often looking behind him, and soon had a procession of thousands of mice walking behind him. When he arrived at the docks at Leith, he threw the brass mouse into the water. All the mice leapt over the edge after the figurine, and drowned.

In a daze the fellow made his way back to the antique shop. When he entered the owner gave him a knowing look and said, 'So, you have come back for the story, sur?'

'Not really. I was wondering is you had any wee brass MSPs!'

Ha Ha Ha!

It was First Minister's Question time and a SNP member stated, 'First Minister, the problem seems to be that you don't understand poor people.'

'Aye, ah do,' came the reply, 'provided they speak slowly!'

Ha Ha Ha!

Two Labour MSPs were in a sauna in Edinburgh. 'Tell me,' said one of them to the other, 'have you read Marx?'

'Aye, ah think it's these wicker chairs.'

Ha Ha Ha!

'Oh, Jonathan,' said an MSP, 'I've decided to make a New Year's resolution.'

'And what's that resolution, Fergus?' replied Jonathan.

'To be much less conceited.'

'And will that be difficult to maintain during the year, Fergus?'

'Not for someone as intelligent and good as me!'

Ha Ha Ha!

An MSP woke up in hospital after a complicated operation, and found that the curtains were drawn round the bed and there were no lights on. 'Hey, nurse, he shouted, 'why are all the curtains closed. Is it during the night?'

The nurse replied, 'No, it's just that there's a big fire across the street, and we didn't want you to think the operation was unsuccessful!'

Ha Ha Ha!

A Scot goes into an electrical store and buys the latest voice-activated radio for his car.

He has it installed and is driving along the road. He decides to try it out so he says, 'Classical,' and immediately the radio plays a Mozart Symphony. Then he says,

'Rock', and an Elvis number plays. Just then a couple of motor cyclists cut in at speed right in front of him, and he shouts, 'Dumb Twits!', and immediately the radio changes to First Minister's Question Time!

Ha Ha Ha!

A secretary was leaving the Scottish Parliament offices when she saw an MSP standing by a shredder with a piece of paper in his hand.

'Listen,' said the MSP, 'this is a Top Confidential document. Can you make this thing work?

The secretary switched the machine on, inserted the paper and pressed the start button.

'Smashing,' said the MSP as the paper disappeared inside the machine. 'I just need one copy.'

Ha Ha Ha!

99.9% of Scots are decent, hardworking, law abiding, and honest citizens. But they must accept the blame for electing the other 0.1%!

Ha Ha Ha!

The First Minister and his Cabinet were out in a posh Edinburgh restaurant for dinner. The First Minister ordered steak, well done, with roast potatoes. 'And what about the vegetables, sir?' asked the waiter.

'Oh, they can order for themselves.'

Ha Ha Ha!

The Highland minister was debating with an elder who doubted the miracle of divine chastisement. 'Let me tell you of a remarkable occurrence,' said the minister, 'In today's *Scotsman*, there was an article about a MSP who was struck by lightning while he was telling a lie. Was that a miracle or was that a miracle?' posed the minister.

'I'm no' sure, meenister,' replied the elder. 'It wid be more of a miracle if lightning struck a MSP when he wasn't lying!'

Ha Ha Ha!

Two Scots were talking. 'You know, Hamish,' said one, 'ma fether wis a Socialist, his fether wis a Socialist, an' his fether afore him. So, that's why ah'm a Socialist.'

'But, Duncan,' said the other, 'that's a pathetic argument. I mean, if your fether wis a swindler, and his fether wia a swindler, an his fether afore him wis a swindler. Now, would that mak you a swindler?'

'Naw, that wid make me a MSP!'

Ha Ha Ha!

The MSP was addressing a meeting of his constituents in a Highland village hall.

'We will cut down on Government overtaxing the people,' he said.

'Aye, an' when will this happen?' came a voice from the hall.

Ignoring the heckler, the MSP continued, 'We will cut down on bureaucracy in Scottish Government and make things more efficient.'

'Aye, an' when will this happen?' came the voice once more.

At this the MSP reckoned he had to deal with the heckler. 'Do you work on a farm by any chance?' he asked. 'Aye.'

'Well, suppose you had a young, virile bull, and you put him in a field with cows, you would get excellent results, but you would not expect to see these results the next morning, would you?'

'Naw, but next morning ah wid expect to see a lot more contented faces than ah see here the night!'

Ha Ha Ha!

Three Edinburgh surgeons were comparing notes. The first surgeon said, 'I think that Scottish librarians are the easiest to operate on. You open them up and everything is in alphabetical order.'

The second surgeon said, 'Sorry, but I beg to differ. I prefer Scottish engineers. They always understand why you have parts left over at the end.'

The third surgeon said, 'I'm afraid you are both wrong. The best patients to operate on are MSPs. They have no brains to start with, they have no morals, and their elbows and rear ends are interchangeable!'

Ha Ha Ha!

At a party a guest said to another, 'Have you heard the latest joke about the First Minister?'

The other replied. 'Before you say anything, I must tell you I work in the First Minister's Office.'

'That's okay,' replied the other, 'I'll tell it slowly and not use big words.'

Ha Ha Ha!

The MSP was going for the 12.30 shuttle to London, but he was troubled with wind. After a visit to the gents at the airport, he noticed a new weighing machine. On it there was a large notice which stated, 'This machine gives your weight and personal details for one pound.' He stuck a pound coin in the machine and a voice said, 'You are 14 stone, seven pounds. You like football, are a MSP, and are on the 12.30 shuttle.'

The MSP was amazed but was unfortunately overcome once more with wind, and disappeared into the gents toilet.

When he came out he thought he would just try this new fangled machine again. The voice boomed out, 'You are 14 stone, seven pounds. You like football, are a MSP, and are on the 12.30 shuttle.'

Just then the MSP was conscious of wind building up again and ran into the gents. When he eventually came out he thought he would just try this wonder machine for the last time. The voice boomed out, 'You are 14 stones, seven pounds. You like football, are a MSP, and with all this farting around you've missed the 12.30 shuttle!'

Ha Ha Ha!

A MSP was in bed with his wife when there was an almighty thunderstorm. A huge bolt of lightning hit nearby and lit up the whole bedroom. The MSP woke up shouting, 'I'll buy the negatives. I'll buy the negatives!'

Ha Ha Ha!

Two wee boys were chatting in the playground of a well-known public school in Edinburgh. 'Hey, did I tell you.

Mummy is getting married again and I'll have a new Daddy.'

'Oh,' said the other boy. 'And who is she marrying?'

'Malcolm MacDuff, the MSP.'

The first boy smiled. 'Oh, you'll like him. He was my Daddy last year!'

Ha Ha Ha!

A man notices that his friend's car is covered in blood, bashes, scrapes, mud, grass and leaves.

'Hey, whit happened to your car?' he asked.

'Well,' the friend replied. 'I ran into a MSP.'

'OK, that explains the blood. But what about all the rest of the stuff on your car?'

'Well, I had to chase him through a park!'

Ha Ha Ha!

Apparently, it's easy to tell in the Scottish Parliament when MSPs have been smoking dope.

They stand almost motionless, stare straight ahead, and speak in boring, dull monotones.

Ha Ha Ha!

The MSP spent a night of wild abandonment in a hotel with a prostitute. In the morning he took out his wallet and laid a hundred pounds on the table.

'Thanks very much,' she replied. 'But I only charge 20.'

'Twenty pounds for an entire night. You can't make much of a living on that.'

'Oh, don't worry. I do a wee bit o' blackmail on the side.'

Ha Ha Ha!

The First minister received a call from 10 Downing Street. 'First Minister, I wonder if you Scots could do us a favour? There has been a major fire at England's largest condom manufacturing plant. Could you possibly get one of your factories to turn out ten million for the English market. All ten inches long and five inches in diameter.'

'Absolutely no problem,' replied the First Minister. 'You know we Scots are always ready to assist our southern neighbours.'

The First Minister immediately phoned the Chief Executive Officer of the Scottish condom plant. 'Could you immediately manufacture ten million condoms, all ten inches long and five inches diameter, for the English market.'

'Of course, First Minister,' replied the CEO.

'Oh, and by the way,' said the First Minister. 'Please print "Made in Scotland – Small Size" on each one.'

Ha Ha Ha!

The Scottish Parliament is unique. It is a place where MSPs get up to speak, talk at length, say nothing, nobody listens ... and then they all disagree and go to the pub!

Ha Ha Ha!

As the MSP's wife bent down to retune the car radio, she felt a sharp pain in her back. 'I think I'm getting lumbago,' she said.

'Turn it off,' said the politician, 'I'm sure we wouldn't understand a word they said anyway!'

Ha Ha Ha!

In order to procure business a contractor offered a MSP a new Rolls Royce. 'Sorry,' said the MSP, 'but we have a very strict ethics code at the Scottish Parliament.'

'Well, sir. I must say I respect your integrity. How would it be if I sold you a Rolls Royce for a thousand pounds?'

The MSP thought for a moment before replying, 'Yes, I'll take two!'

Ha Ha Ha!

An elderly woman called at her MSP's surgery. She informed him that she was a solitary individual who didn't like to go out. She had put aside £5000 for funeral expenses, and was left with £1000 of her savings. As she had never been married and had never slept with a man, she wondered if he could arrange for her to sleep with a nice man. The MSP told her that it was a most unusual request, but as she was a constituent he would see what he could do.

That evening the MSP told his wife about this eccentric old lady and her weird request. His wife thought about it for a minute, then told him he himself should provide the service, after all they could do with a new carpet. 'In fact,' she said, 'I'll drive you over to her house in the morning and wait outside for you.'

The following morning she waited for over two hours before impatiently blowing the horn of the car. Shortly an upstairs window opened, the MSP stuck his head out and shouted, 'Pick me up tomorrow, she's decided to let the Social Security bury her!'

Ha Ha Ha!

A new MSP took his seat in the Scottish Parliament yesterday. The police forced him to put it back!

Ha Ha Ha!

An old woman rang 999: 'Quick, get me the police! There's a labour MSP playing with himself in my garden.'

'And how come you know he's a Labour MSP?' asked the operator.

'Because if he wis a Tory MSP he'd be screwing somebody!'

Ha Ha Ha!

A woman was working on her crossword on the Edinburgh to Glasgow train. There was one word that, although she had pencilled in an answer, she wasn't sure if it was correct. So she asked the man sitting beside her if he could help. 'I need a four letter word ending in IT and the clue is, "something that MSPs are full of and is also found on roads".' The man thought for a minute and then said, 'It must be GRIT.'

'Thanks,' said the lady. 'You wouldn't have an eraser on you by any chance?'

Ha Ha Ha!

One MSP to another, 'I have got to say, you are looking terrific this weather.'

'Don't tell the First Minister,' whispered the other, 'but I'm having an affair.'

'Great! And who's doing the catering?'

Ha Ha Ha!

A luxury bus filled with MSPs was speeding along a Highland road when it hit a tree, ploughed into a field and overturned. There was glass and blood everywhere. An old Highland farmer was first on the scene. He brought up his mechanical digger and buried all the MSPs.

The following day the police spotted the crashed bus and the farmer explained what had happened.

'So, they were all dead?' enquired the police.

'Well,' said the farmer, 'some of them said they weren't, but you know what MSPs are like.'

Ha Ha Ha!

'This is the Scottish Morning News. We have some bad news and good news for the people of Scotland. The bad news is that during the night we were invaded by aliens. The good news is that they eat MSPs and pee whisky.'

Ha Ha Ha!

A MSP retired to a wee bit of land he had in the Highlands. The plan was to turn part of the land into a shooting moor and for that he needed some guidance from the local factor.

'Well, the first thing you'll need is a wee privy for the convenience of your guests, sir. Would you be wanting a single-seater or a two-seater?'

'I'll think it over and let you know later, Jock'

'Would it be wooden seats or plastic seats, sir?'

'I'll think it over and let you know later, Jock'

'And where would you like it located, sir?'

'I'll think it over and let you know later, Jock'

A year later the MSP called his factor. 'Eh, Angus, I was just thinking about that privy and …'

'Och, sir, I built it long ago.'

'Heavens! And is it a single-seater or a two-seater you've built?'

'Och, I made it a single seater, as you'd never make up your mind which hole tae sit oan!'

Ha Ha Ha!

A women went to the doctor. 'I've got very bad news for you,' he said. 'I'm afraid you only have six months to live.'

'Is there anything I can do, doctor?' she asked anxiously.

'Well, you could marry a MSP and go and live in Cumbernauld.'

'Will that cure me, doctor?'

'No, but it'll make it seem like a long time!'

Ha Ha Ha!

The Scottish Country Dance class was being introduced to a new dance. 'Right, listen everyone,' said the dance teacher. 'This one's called the "Scottish Politician". It's really very simple. All you have to do when the music starts is take three steps forward, two steps backward, then side-step, side-step and turn.'

Ha Ha Ha!

A Tory MSP and a Labour MSP were chatting. 'You know,' said the Tory MSP, 'I never pass up a chance to promote the party. For instance, whenever I take a taxi, I give the driver a good tip and say, "Vote Tory".'

The Labour MSP replied, 'Actually I have a much better way of doing it. Whenever I take a taxi, I don't give the driver any tip whatsoever, and I say, "Vote Tory"!'

Ha Ha Ha!

Kilts, Bagpipes and Stuff!

A piper parked his car in an unfashionable part of Glasgow, forgetting he had left his bagpipes in the back-seat and a window open.

When he remembered his oversight he rushed back to the car, but unfortunately it was too late.

There were another three sets on the backseat!

Ha Ha Ha!

The doorbell rang, and McTavish discovered a man complete with a large box of tools, on the doorstep.

'I'm the bagpipe tuner.'

'But ah didnae send for a bagpipe tuner,' protested McTavish.

'No, but your neighbours did.'

Ha Ha Ha!

Q. What's the difference between a bagpipe and an onion?

A. No-one cries when you chop up a bagpipe.

Ha Ha Ha!

Q. What's the difference between a lawn-mower and a set of bagpipes?

A. The owners of a lawn-mower are upset if you don't return it.

Ha Ha Ha!

Q. What's the definition of a Scottish gentleman?

A. Someone who knows how to play the bagpipes, but doesn't.

Ha Ha Ha!

Q. What's the definition of an optimistic Scotsman?
A. A piper with a mobile phone in his pocket.

Ha Ha Ha!

Q. What is the difference between a dead hedgehog on the road and a dead piper on the road?
A. There are skid marks in front of the hedgehog.

Ha Ha Ha!

Q. What is the range of a set of bagpipes?
A. About 30 yards if you have a strong arm.

Ha Ha Ha!

Q. Why are the fingers of pipers like lightning?
A. They never strike the same spot twice.

Ha Ha Ha!

Q. What do you call a piper without a girlfriend?
A. Homeless!

Ha Ha Ha!

Q. What do you call someone who hangs out with pipers?
A. A piper!

Ha Ha Ha!

Q. How do you know you have a piper at your front door?
A. Can't find the key. Doesn't know when to come in!

Ha Ha Ha!

'The bagpipe is the instrument of God, for in its sounding we sense the majesty of the Almighty, and in its ending we know the Grace of the Almighty.'

Ha Ha Ha!

Wee Sandy had moved to London. Visited by a friend from Scotland he was asked how he was doing.

'Weel,' he said, 'it's jist grand here, apart fae they English neighbours. The lot next door scream and shout, and doonstairs is forever knocking up wi a broom.'

'For goodness sake, Sandy, how do you stand all this commotion?' asked his friend.

'Och, ah jist keep quietly practicing on ma pipes!'

Ha Ha Ha!

The Old Scot in America was dying. He was asked by his doctor if he had any last requests. 'Yes. I'd like tae hear the sound o' the pipes afore ah pass over.' A piper was duly summoned, and he marched up and down the ward playing a medley of Highland airs.

In the morning the old Scot felt much better, dressed and went home. All the other patients were dead!

Ha Ha Ha!

An American visiting Scotland for the first time got on a train and sat near a couple of Scottish salesmen. One of these said to the other, 'Been anywhere interesting lately?'

'Aye, I've been to Kilmacolm, Kilmarnock, Kilmichael and Kilsyth. And what aboot yersell?'

'Oh, I've been to Kinmun, Killin and I'm off to Kilmore.'

'Ah knew the Scots were tough but I didn't realise they were all hit-men,' thought the American, and quickly got off at the next stop.

Ha Ha Ha!

People in Largs have to pay large premiums on their car insurance. They must be insured against fire, theft and Viking raids!

Ha Ha Ha!

A Scotsman was fined for indecent conduct at Bute Highland Games. According to many reliable lady witnesses, the man continually wiped the sweat off his brow with his kilt.

Ha Ha Ha!

An Australian was touring Scotland. 'Of course,' he said to a local, 'we have perfect weather in Oz.'

'Heavens!' exclaimed the Scot, 'so what on earth do you have to talk about?'

Ha Ha Ha!

An American arrives in the Highlands of Scotland. It is just as he had imagined it. Mountains tipped with snow, lovely glens, burns, distilleries, and the continual drone of the bagpipes.

When he gets to his hotel he asks the porter if the pipes played all the time.

'Och aye,' replied the porter, 'they play day and night. If the pipes stop then it's very bad news.'

When he comes down to dinner that night he could still hear the pipes. He asks the waitress, 'Do the pipes ever stop?'

'Och no, sur,' she replies, 'if the pipes stop then it's very bad news.'

That evening in the bar he asks the barman, 'Do these bagpipes ever stop?'

'Och no, sur,' replies the barman, 'if the pipes stop then it's very bad news.'

'You know, barman,' says the American, 'you're the third person who has told me that. Why is it such bad news if the bagpipes stop?'

'Well, sur, if you must know, if the bagpipes stop the accordions start!'

Ha Ha Ha!

Someone asks a German how he likes Scottish Punch. 'It's a contradiction,' he replied.

'What do you mean, a contradiction?'

'Well, first of all you put plenty of whisky in it to make it strong. Then you add water to make it weak. Then you add sugar to make it sweet, and then some lemon to make it sour. Then Scots say, "Here's to you," and drink it themselves!'

Ha Ha Ha!

Charlie was told by his late father that there was a tradition in their family. Like his father and grandfather before him, come his 18th birthday, he had to don his kilt, play the bagpipes, and walk over the loch to the hostelry and drink his first dram.

When his 18th birthday arrived he duly put on his best kilt, and playing the bagpipes set off for the loch and the hostelry. Five minutes later he was back in the house, soaked to the skin and shivering wet. 'How did you get into that bedraggled state?' asked his mother. The young man explained the family tradition his father had told him of.

'Ya fool!' said his mother. 'Yer fether and his fether were born in January. Your birthday's in July!'

Ha Ha Ha!

The young man, dressed in full Highland regalia, was at a ceilidh. Although he danced with a number of girls there was one particular girl he really fancied ... in the worst possible way.

After the last dance of the night, the young lady came over and asked if he would like to walk her home.

'Aye, ah would. But how could ye tell ah fancied you? Was it ma look that ye took?'

'Och, no,' she replied. 'It wis the tilt in yer kilt!'

Ha Ha Ha!

A young tourist arrived late at a small hotel in the Highlands.

After some dinner the couple who owned the establishment bade him good night, but warned him, 'Mak sure ye lock yer door before ye go tae sleep, as oor lassie walks in her sleep.'

The young man was immediately aroused and deliberately left his bedroom door open.

In the middle of the night he was wakened by a tongue licking his lips. He opened his eyes to see Lassie, an old sheepdog.

Ha Ha Ha!

The Polis!

How many Scottish police does it take to break an egg?
None. It fell down the stairs!

Ha Ha Ha!

A policeman spotted a woman driving and knitting at the same time.
'Pull over, madam,' he shouted.
'Naw, officer, it's jist a pair o' socks!'

Ha Ha Ha!

A member of the public went to his local police station, and asked to see the burglar who had broken into his house recently.
'Sorry, sir,' replied the desk sergeant, 'but I cannot allow you to see him. Anyway, you'll get your chance in court.'
'But you dinnae understand, officer,' replied the man. 'I want tae know how to get intae ma hoose in the middle of the night without waking the wife!'

Ha Ha Ha!

A policeman stopped a motorist in the centre of a Scottish town. 'Excuse me, sur, but would you mind blowing into this bag?'
'Why, officer?' asked the motorist.
'Ma chips are too hot!'

Ha Ha Ha!

A police recruit was being questioned by a panel of senior officers. 'If you were all alone in a patrol car, and were being pursued by a gang of criminals doing 70 miles an hour through a twisting road in a Highland glen, what would you do?'

'Eighty, sur!'

Ha Ha Ha!

Two Scottish magistrates were booked for speeding and as they were friends they agreed to try each other. So the following day one sat on the bench and the other in the dock. A plea of 'not guilty' was entered, and after all the evidence was heard the case was found 'not proven'. Then the magistrates changed places.

The second magistrate also pleaded 'not guilty', but after hearing the evidence his friend pronounced him 'guilty' and fined him £500, telling the court that this was the second case of speeding to come before the court that morning, and that he was determined to stamp it out!

Ha Ha Ha!

Looking down at the poor defendant in the dock, the judge in the High Court in Glasgow said, 'MacDonald, taking everything into consideration, I've decided to give you a suspended sentence.'

'Oh, thank you, thank you,' cried MacDonald.

'I sentence you to be hanged!'

Ha Ha Ha!

The two new prisoners had just been shown to their cell. 'Hoo many years are you in fur?' asked the first one.

'Ten years.'

'Aye, well ah'm in fur 15, so you take the bed nearest the door since you're getting oot first.'

Ha Ha Ha!

A new policeman was out in a patrol car in Perth with a somewhat more experienced policeman, when they saw a group of people loitering on the pavement.

'Don't worry,' exclaimed the young policeman excitedly, 'I'll handle this just fine.'

'Right folks, move along, please. Have you not got homes to go to?' he told the gathering.

The people slowly dispersed in different directions.

The young constable climbed back into the patrol car. 'So, what did you think of that?' he asked his companion. 'Was that good or was that good?'

'Aye,' replied the older policeman reluctantly, 'you did okay. Only one wee problem. It *was* the bus queue for Pitlochry!'

Ha Ha Ha!

'Right, sur,' said the policeman on Princes Street, 'do you have permission to play the accordion in the street?'

'Naw!'

'In that case, sur,' said the policeman, 'I'll have to ask you to accompany me.'

'Nae problem, officer. Dae ye know, "Ah'm No' Awa Tae Bide Awa"?'

Ha Ha Ha!

The Judge at the High Court said to the prisoner. 'I sentence you to be hanged, and I hope you'll never do such a terrible crime again!'

Ha Ha Ha!

On a remote Highland road a police officer, holding a radar gun, stopped a motorist for speeding. Looking in the car he noticed a dog in the back.

'Does yer dog have a licence?' asked the policeman.

'Och no, officer,' replied the motorist, 'I do all the driving masell!'

Ha Ha Ha!

The motorist parked in the town car park, and as he was getting out of his car he was approached by a plain-clothes policeman.

'Will you be parking for long?' asked the policeman.

'And why would you be wanting to know?' queried the motorist.

'Well, I'm a policeman.'

'Well you don't look like a policeman tae me,' said the man. 'In fact you're wearing a sports jacket.'

'That's right, sur. This is a routine check!'

Ha Ha Ha!

The prosecution and the defence lawyers had both presented their final speeches in a case involving a Highlander operating an illegal whisky still. The judge turned to the jury and said, 'Now before my final summing up, are there any questions?'

'Yes, sir,' said one of the jury members. 'Did the defendant boil the malt for two or three hours, how long does it take to cool, and at what point did he add the yeast?'

Ha Ha Ha!

A wee boy approached a policeman in Braehead shopping centre.

'Excuse me, mister, but huv ye seen a wummin withoot a wee boy like me?'

Ha Ha Ha!

The magistrate in a Glasgow courthouse addressed the prisoner in the dock.

'Jimmy McGinty, you are charged with the crime of theft. Do you plead guilty or not guilty?'

'Ah don't know yet, sur. Ah'll jist wait tae see how good the evidence is!'

Ha Ha Ha!

The drunk was making a terrible noise wandering round a car park, bumping into cars and then feeling their roofs. A passer-by stopped and asked, 'Can ah help ye, pal?'

'Ah'm looking fur ma car an' ah cannae find it,' replies the drunk.

'And why are you feeling all the car roofs?' asks the passer-by.

'Well,' says the drunk, 'ma car has two blue lights and a wee siren oan the roof!'

Ha Ha Ha!

One night a police car stopped a motorist driving up the Rest-and-be-Thankful. 'Do you realize, sur, that you are driving without a rear light?'

The driver got out of the car, ran to the rear and started to cry.

'There, there, sur,' said the policemen, 'it's only a minor offence.'

'That may be so,' sobbed the man, 'but where's ma bloody caravan?'

Ha Ha Ha!

The young policeman stopped a stranger, 'Ye'll need tae accompany me tae the station, sir.'

'But why, officer?'

'Because it's awfa dark an' ah'm frightened tae go there on ma own!'

Ha Ha Ha!

Sheriff Campbell had called the opposing lawyers into his chambers. 'So,' he said, 'both of you have given me a bribe.' The lawyers looked at each other and squirmed. 'You, Mister Shields, gave me £3000. And as for you, Mister McConnell, you gave me £2000.'

The Sheriff reached inside his jacket and pulled out a cheque. He handed it to Shields. 'Now then, Mr Shields, I'm returning £1000. We're going to decide this case solely on its merits!'

Ha Ha Ha!

The motorist was pulled over by a Highland bobby who proceeded to check the man's licence.

'It states in yer licence, sur, that ye must wear glasses.'

'But, officer, I have contacts.'

'Ah dinnae care whether you know the Chief Constable himsell, ah'm bookin' ye!'

Ha Ha Ha!

The magistrate concluded his sentencing of the old offender by saying, 'And I hope this is the last time you'll appear before me.'

'Why's that, sur,' replied the prisoner. 'Ur ye retiring?'

Ha Ha Ha!

Late one night in Edinburgh, a police car was following a car containing a man and his wife. The driver of the car drove very well, never going over the speed limit, never going through red lights, always being courteous to other road users.

Eventually the patrol car pulled alongside and stopped the motorist. 'Excuse me, sur,' said the policeman, 'you're not in any trouble whatsoever. In fact we just want to congratulate you on your exemplary driving.'

The man's wife leaned over and said, 'Aye, he always makes a point of driving carefully when he's had a few drams.'

Ha Ha Ha!

A group of cars were speeding their way north on the A9 towards Inverness when one was stopped as it went through a police radar trap.

When the policeman approached the car, the driver said indignantly, 'Look officer, I know I was speeding, but I don't think it is fair. There were plenty of cars all around me going just as fast as me!'

'Ever go fishing on the River Spey?' asked the policeman.

'Aye, sometimes,' replied the driver.

'Did ye ever catch all the fish?'

Ha Ha Ha!

A man was approached in the street. 'Excuse me, but are there any policeman around here?'

'You must be joking. You can never find one around here!'

'Oh, good. Stick 'em up, pal!'

Ha Ha Ha!

A man was caught breaking into a house and was brought before the Justice of the Peace. 'What will you take?' asked the JP. 'Thirty days or three hundred pounds?'

'Ah'll jist take the money!'

Ha Ha Ha!

A motorist was charged with speeding at 90 miles per hour on the M8 motorway.

'But, your honour,' he pleaded, 'I wasn't doing 90.'

'Were you doing 75?' asked the Justice of the Peace.

'No, sir.'

'Were you doing 50?'

'No, sir.'

'Were you doing 20?'

'No, sir.'

'Oh, for heavens sake!' said the JP. 'Fined two hundred pounds for parking on a motorway!'

Ha Ha Ha!

An old Scotsman woke up one night to hear voices from downstairs. He looked over the banister and saw a couple of burglars ransacking the house. The Scot immediately phoned the police and explained the situation. 'Sorry, sir, but it will be an hour or so before we get to you as we're busy at present.'

The old man put down the phone for a minute, then redialled the police. 'Forget it,' he informed them, 'I've just shot them.'

Two minutes later three police cars plus an armed response unit came round the corner. The burglars were quickly apprehended.

'Hey,' said the Police inspector, 'I thought you said you had shot them?'

'Aye, an' ah thought you said you lot were too busy tae come!'

Ha Ha Ha!

A policeman approached a motorist sitting in his car. 'Is this car licensed, sur?'

'Of course it is,' replied the motorist.

'Right then,' said the policeman, 'I'll have a whisky.'

Ha Ha Ha!

The Glasgow lawyer was leading his witness. 'What state were you in on the night in question?' he asked.

'Drunk as a Judge.'

At this the Judge intervened. 'Don't you mean, "As drunk as a Lord", my good fellow?'

'Aye, ma Lord!'

Ha Ha Ha!

An old Scot decided that as everybody else seemed to be shoplifting, he would try it too. So, although he had led a blameless life, he visited the local Tescos to try his luck.

He moved from aisle to aisle deciding what he would take and eventually opted for half-a-dozen apples. But the CCTV cameras picked him up and the police were called. Soon he found himself at the local Sheriff Court.

'Is this your first offence?' asked the Sheriff.

'Aye, sir, it is.'

'Unfortunately, irrespective of your age, we have to deal with such things in accordance with the law. It was 6 apples you stole, was it not?'

'Aye, sir.'

'Well, even although you are a pensioner, I am going to have to sentence you to a week in jail for each apple. Have you anything to say?'

'Aye, sir. It's a bloody good job ah pit that tin o' peas back!'

Ha Ha Ha!

The Workplace

A man walked into a branch of the Bank of Scotland and went up to the counter.

'May I help you, sir,' asked the teller.

'Aye. Ah want tae open a bloody bank account in this bloody bank!'

'I'm very sorry, sir, but I couldn't possibly open a bank account for someone who uses such language. Please hold on a moment and I'll get the manager.'

'What seems to be the problem, sir,' asked the bank manager.

'It's simple, pal. Ah want tae open a bloody bank account in this bloody bank, wi the bloody ten million ah jist won on the bloody Lotto!'

'Oh, I see,' said the bank manager. 'And is this bloody teller giving you bloody hassle, sir?'

Ha Ha Ha!

A vendor at the Glasgow Barrows was selling fresh seagulls at £2 each. A chap went up to him, handed over his money and said. 'I'll have one please.'
The vendor pointed to a seagull flying in the sky above them. 'Ok pal, ye can huv that wan!'

Ha Ha Ha!

Three elderly Scots were talking, over a dram, about what their grandchildren would be saying about them in 50 years.

'I would like my grandchildren to say,' said one 'that I was a highly successful Scottish businessman.'

'Well,' said the second. 'I would like them to say I was an extremely successful Scottish businessman.'

The third Scot then piped up: 'I would like them to say, "Doesn't he look just grand for his age"!'

Ha Ha Ha!

Jimmy, from Glasgow, decided to go into the business of training greyhounds. He bought a greyhound but sadly, it died before it could race.

A few months later he met a pal, Wullie, who said he was very sorry to hear that his greyhound business had failed when the dog died.

'Nut at all, Wullie,' replied Jimmy. 'That dug made me a fortune.'

'How did you manage that?' asked the astonished Wullie.

'I organised a raffle with the dog as the prize and sold thousands of tickets at five pounds each.'

'Raffle a deed dug? You must have got nothing but complaints.'

'Only from the fella that won. And I gave him his five pounds back!'

Ha Ha Ha!

The Town Council put out tenders for a wall to be built. Only three tenders were received by the Provost, so he decided to interview them all.

The first builder gave a tender of £3,000: £1,000 for him, £1,000 for materials and £1,000 for the workmen.

The second builder put forward a tender of £6,000: £2,000 for him, £2,000 for materials and £2,000 for the workmen.

The third builder gave his tender of £9,000, but didn't give a breakdown of the costs.

'Okay,' said the provost, 'here's whit we'll do. I'll give £3,000 to you, £3,000 to masell, and I'll give the job tae the first tender!'

Ha Ha Ha!

A man was on a tour of a Scottish factory that produced various rubber products. On the assembly line he was shown the machinery that manufactures baby-bottle teats. The machine made a 'hiss-pop' sound.

'The hiss is the rubber being injected into the mould,' explained the operator. 'The popping is the needle poking a hole in the tip of the teat.'

Later, the tour took in the equipment that produced condoms. The machine here made a 'hiss, hiss, hiss, pop' sound

'I understand what the "hiss" sound means,' said the man. 'But why the "pop" every so often?

'Och, sur, it's a wee bit like the baby teat machine,' said the operator, 'but here the needle pokes a hole in every third condom.'

'Well, that can't be good for the condom business,' observed the man.

'Yer right, sur,' replied the operator, 'but it's gey good for the teat business.'

Ha Ha Ha!

'This car you sold me is useless,' complained the irate customer to the Highland garage owner.

'And what would be the matter with it, sur,'

'The first week one of the doors fell off, then all the electrics went, the exhaust blew, the steering wheel came off in my hand, and today it just won't start. I thought you said it had only one careful lady owner.'

'That I did, but the other five were not quite as careful.'

Ha Ha Ha!

Every time the ferry chugged its way across the Clyde, the old master of the Govan Ferry was observed pulling a small black notebook from the inside pocket of his jacket. The crew speculated on the book's contents over many years. Some thought it contained the names of women friends, and others thought it must be on the horses – after all, the captain was known to enjoy an occasional flutter.

One day, halfway across, the Captain suddenly had a heart attack and died. As the shocked crew awaited a doctor and undertaker, the First Mate took it upon himself to slip the well-worn black notebook from the Captain's pocket. Opening it he found a single entry, 'Port left, Starboard right.'

Ha Ha Ha!

A tourist drove into a deep ditch beside a road in the Highlands. Luckily a farmer and his old Clydesdale horse came along. 'Don't you worry. Billy will pull your car out the ditch.'

Soon the car was hitched up to the horse and the farmer shouted, 'Pull, Dobbin, pull!' Billy didn't move.

Then the farmer yelled. 'Pull, Dolly, pull!' Billy didn't move.

The farmer then shouted at the top of his voice. 'Pull, Nellie, pull!' Billy still didn't move.

Then the farmer said in a low voice. 'Pull, Billy, pull.' Billy dutifully pulled the car out of the ditch.

The tourist was most appreciative, but asked why the farmer had called his horse the wrong name three times.

'Well, sur, ye see Billy is a very stubborn horse. But he's also blind – if he thought he was the only one pulling he wouldn't even try.'

Ha Ha Ha!

'How long have you been working here, Hamish?' asked his boss.
'Ever since they threatened tae sack me!'

Ha Ha Ha!

A Scotsman had a terrible accident at work and lost his manhood.

Eventually he saw a private consultant who advised him that a small replacement could be obtained for £2,000. A larger version would be £5,000. A top-of-the-range version was available for £14,000.

'Fourteen thoosan' poon is an awfa lot o' money,' said the man. 'I'll need tae go hame and talk it o'er wi' the wife.'

A week later the man revisited the consultant. 'Well, what's the decision?' the consultant asked.
'Wur getting a new kitchen!'

Ha Ha Ha!

A man in Glasgow saw an advert for a handyman. He applied and got an interview.

'How are you at joinery work?' asked the interviewer.
'Useless.'
'How are you at plumbing?' asked the interviewer.
'Nae good.'
'How are you at painting?'
'Pathetic.'

'So why do you think you're handy?'
'Ah live jist roon the corner!'

Ha Ha Ha!

'Excuse me, sir,' said a Glasgow man to his boss, 'can I have tomorrow off to do some shopping with my wife, her mother and our five children.'

'Certainly not! We are far too busy to let you off.'

'Oh, thanks, sur. Ye're so kind and understanding.'

Ha Ha Ha!

A man went to see his boss. 'Listen, sur,' he said, 'as you know ah'm wan o' yer best workers an' ah wonder if ah could hae a rise?'

'Well, McKinnon, an employee's true worth is based on how he would fare on the job market.'

'Well, sur', replied McKinnon, 'I'll have you know there are four companies after me.'

'Oh, and just who may they be?' asked the boss.

'Scottish Power, Scottish Gas, BT and ma credit card company!'

Ha Ha Ha!

A tourist went to a restaurant advertising: 'All You Can Eat For £1.50.'

The tourist filled up his plate, gobbled it all down and went back for more.

The big Scottish manager took his plate and growled, 'That's aw ye can eat fur one pound 50!'

Ha Ha Ha!

Scottish
Education

'What's the opposite of joy?' asked a Glasgow teacher of her class.

'Sadness, miss,' came the reply.

'Very good. Now what's the opposite of happiness?'

'Depression, miss.'

'Very good. Now what's the opposite of woe?'

'Giddy up, miss.'

Ha Ha Ha!

'And where are you from?' the teacher demanded of a new pupil in her class.

'Glesca, miss.'

'Which part?'

'The whole lot o' me, miss.'

Ha Ha Ha!

A teacher was telling her third-year class that they had to pay five pounds to get a copy of the class photograph. 'You know, this will mean so much to you in 40 years time,' she said. 'You'll look at it and say, there's Joe MacDuff, he's a lawyer, there's Maggie McDonald, she's a doctor, and there's …'

A voice from the back of the class suddenly interrupted '… and there's oor teacher, Miss McFadden, she's deed!'

Ha Ha Ha!

Wee Sammy was forever turning up late for school in the morning, but as he was the son of a local farmer, and the teacher knew that farm tasks had to be shared in the family, then she made allowances for Sammy. One day Sammy slipped into his desk two hours late.

'So why are you so late today, Sammy?' asked the teacher.

'I'm very sorry, miss,' said Sammy, 'but I hud tae see tae ma duties roon the farm.'

'And what was the very special duty that made you so late this morning, may I ask,' she demanded.

'Well, ye see miss. Ah hud tae take the bull doon tae the coos.'

'But surely you father could have done that,' said the teacher.

'Och no, miss,' explained Sammy, 'It has tae be the bull.'

Ha Ha Ha!

'Let's do spelling this morning,' the teacher announced to her class.

'Dougal. How do you spell 'farm'?'

'E-I-E-I-O, miss.'

Ha Ha Ha!

'Now listen carefully, class,' said the teacher, 'it's a very interesting linguistic fact that, in English, a double negative forms a positive. In some languages, like Russian, a double negative is still a negative. However, there is no language in which a double positive can form a negative.'

'Aye, right, Miss!'

Ha Ha Ha!

A lecturer was invigilating for an exam at a college that he didn't work at. Before the exam started he told the students that it would last one hour, and as soon as he said'Stop!' everyone had to put down their pens or their papers would not count.

At the end of the exam, one student kept writing on the exam paper for a couple of minutes after they were told to stop. Then he got up and strode confidently to the front to turn it in.

The Lecturer said, 'Don't bother to hand that paper in, young man. You get nothing for writing after I told you to stop.'

'Do you know who I am, sir?' asked the student.

'Listen,' replied the lecturer, 'I don't care if you're the son of the University Principal, you get nothing in this exam.'

'You mean, sir,' asked the student, 'you have absolutely no idea who I am?'

'None, young man,' said the lecturer. 'In fact I couldn't care less.'

The student then slipped his exam paper into the middle of the stack and ran out.

Ha Ha Ha!

A teacher in the West of Scotland was determined to improve her pupils' grammar. She wanted to get rid of all those 'dids' and 'dones'.

'Mary, give me a sentence beginning with 'I'.'

'I is …'

'Mary, will you never learn. How many times must I tell you? You must always say "I am",' interrupted the teacher.

'Sorry, miss. I am the letter in the alphabet afore H.'

One day, at a school in a rural part of Scotland, the teacher asked the class to think of stories with a moral to them. A hand went up. It was wee Peggy, who said, 'My Dad has a farm and every Saturday we load the chicken eggs on the trailer and drive into the market. Well, one Saturday, we hit a big bump in the road and all the eggs fell out the basket onto the road.'

'So what is the moral of that story?' asked the teacher.

'Don't put all your eggs in one basket,' replied Peggy. 'Very good, Peggy,' said the teacher. 'Now, anyone else?'

Another hand shot up. 'Well,' said wee Mary, 'my Dad has a farm too, and every day we take the chicken eggs and put them in the incubator. Yesterday only 50 of the hundred eggs hatched.'

'So what is the moral of that particular story?' asked the teacher.

'Don't count your chickens before they are hatched,' replied wee Mary.

'Very good, Mary,' said the teacher. 'Now anyone else?'

Another hand shot up. 'Well,' said wee Jimmy, 'my Grandpa was in the war, and his plane was shot down over Germany. When he landed in his parachute all he had with him was a bottle of whisky, a machine-gun and a skean-dhu. Unfortunately he landed in the middle of a German patrol of 30 soldiers. So he drank the bottle of whisky, shot 25 of the enemy before his machine-gun jammed, then finished off the rest with his skean-dhu.'

'So what is the moral of that particular story?' asked the teacher.

'Don't mess around wi ma Grandpa when he's got a good drink in him!'

Ha Ha Ha!

An applicant for Teacher Training was asked to fill in an application form. The first question was: Give two good reasons why you wish to become a teacher. She wrote: 'July and August.'

Ha Ha Ha!

A Glasgow school had a new swimming pool for its pupils. It was filled with 20,000 gallons of water. At the end of the following week it was emptied of 21,000 gallons of water!

Ha Ha Ha!

A wee boy went to school for the first time. When he got home his father asked him how he got on.

'Ah wish ah hudnae goad, paw,' he replied.

His father replied. 'Listen son, it's no' "ah hudnae goad", it's "ah hudnae went".'

'Well, Dad, ah wish tae goad ah hudnae went!'

Ha Ha Ha!

Saint Peter heard a noise outside the Pearly Gates.

'Who is there?' he asked.

'It is I,' came the reply.

'Oh no! Not another Scottish schoolteacher!'

Ha Ha Ha!

Wee Hughie's parents were discussing his progress in school. 'How did Hughie get on in his History exam?' asked his Dad.

'Not very well,' replied his mother, 'but then you cannae really fault him. A lot of these questions were about things that happened afore he was born!'

Ha Ha Ha!

A wee Scottish boy came home from school all excited. He had just got a part in the school play.

'Wonderful, pet. What is it?' asked his mother.

'I've to play the part of a Scottish husband.'

His mother's face fell. 'Jist you get back tae that school right now, and tell them you want a speaking part!'

Ha Ha Ha!

'Dad, will you help me with ma homework?'

'Sorry, son,' replied the father. 'You see, it widnae be right.'

'I know that Dad, but at least you could try.'

Ha Ha Ha!

The English teacher was trying out difficult and unusual words on her second year class. 'Right,' she asked, 'what's inertia?'

'Please, miss, Ayr and Troon!'

Ha Ha Ha!

A woman was walking along a road when she saw a wee boy leaning against a wall, smoking a cigar and sipping from a bottle of whisky. The woman was shocked and demanded, 'Hey, why aren't you at school at this time of day?'

'At school!' replied the boy, taking a long, slow slug from the bottle. 'Listen hen, ah'm only four!'

Ha Ha Ha!

The Scots
at Worship

The decorative border reads "Ha Ha Ha!" repeatedly around the page.

Willie decided to clear up some rough ground at the back of his garden. After many months of work the summer brought a wonderful display of flowers and vegetables.

One day the minister paid him a visit, commenting. 'Well, Willie. I must say that you and the guid Lord have between you done a grand bit of work on this ground.'

'Well, Meenister, maybe so ... but you should have seen the mess o' it when the guid Lord had it tae himsell.'

Ha Ha Ha!

A Scot entered a monastery in the Highlands and had to take a vow of silence. He was told he could only speak once a year, when he came face-to-face with the Father Abbot.

After a year he appeared in front of the Abbot who informed him that, if he wished, he could speak. The chap slowly said, 'Bed ... hard.'

At the end of the following year he appeared in front of the Abbot, and this time when asked to speak, said. 'Food ... bad.'

At the third year-end he was again in front of the Abbot, and when asked if he would like to say something, replied. 'I ... quit.'

'Thank heavens,' said the Abbot. 'You've done nothing but moan since you got here!'

Ha Ha Ha!

The young Scottish minister and his girlfriend were out for a run in his car on a Sunday afternoon. He swung the car into a deserted lay-by and switched off the engine.

'As it's Sunday, my dear, and this is a quiet spot miles from anywhere, I thought we might discuss the hereafter,' he said.

'Oh, right. But why the hereafter?'

'Easy! If you're not hereafter what I'm hereafter, you'll be hereafter I'm gone!'

Ha Ha Ha!

The minister was really getting into his sermon. 'And there shall be much weeping and gnashing of teeth ...'

In the front seat sat old McDougall, and he grinned up challengingly at the minister, displaying a perfect set of gums.

'Dinnae fash yersell,' thundered the minister, 'teeth will be provided!'

Ha Ha Ha!

There were two brothers in Glasgow. Both were evil men, into drugs, racketeering, prostitution and all manner of things.

One of the brothers died, and the other approached the local parish priest to take the service. 'Ah want ma brother tae be well remembered, so if ye agree tae say at his funeral he wis a saint, ah'll give ye five thousand pounds cash right now.' The priest duly agreed. At the funeral service the priest said, 'He was an evil man, a corrupt man, into all kinds of wickedness, but compared to his brother he was a saint!'

Ha Ha Ha!

The minister in a small Scottish town was reported to his Church Board for an indiscretion with his housekeeper. It was alleged his vest had been found in her pantry, and her pants in his vestry!

Ha Ha Ha!

The congregation were shocked when it was announced that their minister had been called to another church.

After the service, a distraught woman came up to the minister with tears sparkling in her eyes. 'Oh, meenister, we are going tae miss ye.'

The minister patted her hand and replied. 'There, there, my dear. The minister who takes my place might even be better than me.'

'Huh,' she said, with a tone of disappointment in her voice, 'that's whit they said the last time!'

Ha Ha Ha!

Old Sandy Mcduff went to church each Sunday. One Sunday there was a new preacher and, right in the middle of the sermon, Old Sandy got up and walked out. Later that day his wee grandson, who had been to church with him, asked, 'Granpaw, why did you leave the church early?'

'The sermon was over, son.'

'I don't think so, Grandpaw. He was only about half-way through. He had preached against mixing with the opposite sex, gambling, and gossiping, and was just starting on the whisky drinking when you got up and left.'

'That's whit I mean, son. He had finished preaching and was starting tae meddle!'

Ha Ha Ha!

The minister of a small Highland church was concerned about the spiritual welfare of a rather gorgeous young widow in his congregation.

As he was shaking hands at the church door after one Sunday service, he said to the widow, 'Last night I prayed for two hours for you.'

Said the widow with a shy smile. 'Goodness, meenister, you needn't have gone to all that trouble. If you had just phoned, I could have been up at the manse in ten minutes.'

Ha Ha Ha!

The minister said to his elder. 'I'm told you were playing football this morning instead of being at the service.'

'That's a lie,' said the elder, 'and here's the salmon to prove it!'

Ha Ha Ha!

'Mum, dae Scotsmen go tae heaven?' asked a wee boy.

'Of course, ma wee pet. But whit are ye askin' fur?'

'Well, ah've never seen ony pictures o' angels wi' beards and whiskers.'

'Well, some of them do get tae heaven, but it's a gey close shave.'

Ha Ha Ha!

Wee Jaimie arrived home from Sunday School eating a bar of chocolate. 'And just where,' demanded his mother, 'did you get the money to buy that?'

'With the 50 pence you gave me.'

'But that was for the Sunday school.'

'Ah know, but the minister met me at the door and got me in for free!'

Ha Ha Ha!

The couple were on their yacht sailing from the Scottish mainland to Orkney.

Suddenly a dreadful storm arrived and the boat was broken up by huge waves.

Sitting in their tiny life raft without food or water, the couple were tossed this way and that for a number of days. On the fourth day, the man started to pray, 'Oh Lord, please save us. Please end this misery on this violent sea. If you save us I will give up the sins of gambling, smoking, swearing, unkind thoughts, and I will even refrain from drinking the whis ...'

He was quickly interrupted by his wife, 'Ye had better stop there, Hamish, ah think ah can see land!'

Ha Ha Ha!

It was the Sabbath afternoon and the minister paid an unannounced visit to one of his elders. 'He's no' in,' announced the small boy who answered the door. 'He's over at the golf course.'

'On the Sabbath?'

'It's okay, meenister, he's no' playing golf. He's just having a couple o' drams and playing some poker wi' his mates.'

Ha Ha Ha!

It was Christmas morning and the McGregor family were trudging their way through the snow, back home from church. As they walked they discussed the service. Mr McGregor thought that the bells for such a special occasion had not been rung well. Mrs McGregor thought that the choice of hymns was inappropriate. The daughter thought that the sermon was too long and boring. Wee McGregor listened then he said. 'Ah don't know whit you're aw moaning aboot. Ah thocht it wis no' a bad show fur ten pence!'

Ha Ha Ha!

A stranger went to a Church of Scotland service, and afterwards he was shaking hands with the minister as he left. 'I've got to tell you, meenister,' he said, 'that wis a damned good sermon. Damned good!'

The minister said, 'Thank you for saying so, but I'd rather you didn't use such language at church.'

'I was so damned impressed with yer sermon, that I put a thousand pounds in the damned collection plate.'

'Well,' said the minister, 'that was damned good of you!'

Ha Ha Ha!

A Scottish atheist was fishing in Loch Ness when Nessie suddenly attacked his boat.

The boat was tipped over and the force threw the man skywards towards the monster's waiting jaws. He suddenly screamed, 'God, save me!'

Suddenly time was frozen and the man was left hanging in mid-air, inches from the monster's fangs. A voice came from the sky. 'I thought you didn't believe in Me!'

'Gies a break, God. Thirty seconds ago ah didnae believe in the Loch Ness Monster!'

Ha Ha Ha!

A young Scot began to go out with a young woman who was a 'Wee Free'.

'Tell me, Jessie,' asked the boy, 'would the "Wee Free" Church allow me to drink coffee?'

'No way,' replied Jessie. 'Coffee beans are treated to enhance their flavour, so we do not consider coffee to be completely natural.'

'What about dancing? Could you and I go to the jiggin'?'

'The "Wee Free" Church does not permit dancing,' replied Jessie. 'It's unnatural.'

'What about sex?'

'Sex is permissible as long as it is between two people that are married.'

'What about kinky sex?'

'What do you mean by kinky sex?'

'Well,' replied the boy, 'I was thinking of different positions, like standing up.'

'No way, that could lead to dancing.'

Ha Ha Ha!

A wee boy and his granny were walking along the sea front at Gourock, when a huge wave appeared out of nowhere and swept the wee boy out to sea.

The granny was horrified. She fell to her knees and prayed, 'Dear Lord, please save ma wee grandson.'

Then another wave swept in and deposited the little boy at her feet. She picked him up, gave him a hug and looked him over. Then she glared up at the sky and shouted, 'Where's his wee tammy ah knitted him?'

Ha Ha Ha!

The Fitba!

The boy said to his girlfriend. 'Hey, we are gonnae have a great time on Saturday. Ah've managed tae get three tickets fur the big game.'

'Three? Whit dae we need three fur?'

'Two fur yer fether an' mother, an' wan fur yer wee sister!'

Ha Ha Ha!

A wee boy got lost at Hampden Park during a match. He went up to one of the policemen. 'Ah've loast ma fether.'

'What's he like?' asked the sympathetic officer.

'Whisky an' fitba'.'

Ha Ha Ha!

Q. What do you call a Scotsman holding the World Cup?
A. A thief!

Ha Ha Ha!

At an Old Firm match things got a bit out of hand and a few cans flew between both sets of supporters. A wee lad was concerned that he might get hit. 'Don't you worry, son,' reassured an older supporter next to him. 'It's like bullets, you only get hit if yer name's on it.'

'That's whit ah'm worried aboot, mister,' replied the youth. 'Ma name's Tennant!'

Ha Ha Ha!

The goalkeeper had let in six soft goals and was moaning to the rest of the players in the dressing room. 'Ye see, ah'm no' weel,' he said. 'Ah think ah've caught a cold.'

'At least yer are able tae catch something!' retorted one of the players.

Ha Ha Ha!

The Scottish second division club was doing well, mainly due to the talents of their teenage striker.

Half-way through the season the young lad was called into the manager's office. 'Ye're doin' well, lad,' exclaimed the manager. 'and here's a wee appreciation from the chairman for aw yer efforts.' He handed over a cheque for ten thousand pounds.

'Wow, thanks, boss,' said the player. 'That'll let me buy a new set o' wheels.'

'Jist wan wee thing,' said the manager. 'The chairman says that if ye score another 25 goals between now an' the end o' the season, he'll sign it fur ye!'

Ha Ha Ha!

A Scottish football widow was annoyed at her husband. 'Your whole life is football, football, football! We never go out anywhere together. You're either at a match, watching one on the telly, or down at the pub discussing football with your mates. I bet you don't even know the date we got married.'

'Of course ah do, ma wee hen. Sure it wis the day that St Mirren beat Aberdeen in the quarter-finals o' the cup!'

Ha Ha Ha!

A Scots woman was reading the adverts in her local newspaper when she spots one that upset her. 'Would you credit this, Tam?' she says. 'Here's some guy has put an advert in the paper offering tae swap his wife for tickets to the Scottish Cup Final. Now you'd never do anything like that, would you, pet?'

'Don't be silly, darling,' says her husband. 'I've already got two tickets fur the game!'

Ha Ha Ha!

One evening Mummy Potato and her three daughters sat down to dinner. Halfway through the meal, the eldest daughter says, 'Mummy Potato, I have an announcement to make.'

'And what might that be,' said Mummy Potato.

'Well,' said the eldest Potato daughter, 'I'm getting married!'

The other daughters squealed with delight and Mummy Potato said, 'Wonderful. I'm so pleased. And who are you marrying, eldest Potato daughter?'

'I'm marrying a King Edward.'

'A King Edward,' repeated the Mummy Potato, 'why a King Edward is a fine tater indeed.'

Suddenly the middle daughter spoke up. 'Mummy Potato, I, too, have an announcement to make.'

'And what might that be,' asked Mummy Potato.

'I am also getting married,' announced the middle Potato daughter.

'You also?' exclaimed Mummy Potato, 'this is indeed a wonderful evening. And who are you marrying, middle daughter?'

'I'm marrying a Jersey,' said the middle daughter.

'A Jersey!' said Mummy Potato hardly able to contain her joy. 'Oh, a Jersey is a fine tater, a fine tater indeed.'

The youngest daughter then coughed and said, 'I too have an announcement to make, Mummy Potato.'

'And what might that be,' asked Mummy Potato with growing excitement.

'I am getting married too, Mummy Potato!'

'Fantastic! All of my girls getting married. And tell me, dear youngest Potato daughter, who are you marrying?'

'I'm marrying Dougie Donnelly, the football man on the telly, Mummy Potato.'

Oh, no!' screamed Mummy Potato, 'but he's just a common tater!'

Ha Ha Ha!

Peter came to his work one Monday morning with a terrible limp. His boss asked him what the problem was. 'Och, it's nothing,' replied Peter. 'Jist an auld fitba' injury.'

'I never knew you played football, Peter,' replied the boss.

'Ah don't. Ah hurt it last week during the Cup Final. When Dundee United scored ah stuck ma fit through the telly!'

Ha Ha Ha!

'You know something, McGrath,' observed his boss. 'It hasnae escaped ma notice that every time there's a mid-week match on, you have to go to your granny's funeral.'

'You know, sur,' said McGrath, 'you're right. Dae ye think she's faking it?'

Ha Ha Ha!

A football fan arrives breathlessly at a football match, halfway through the second half.

'Whit's the score?' he asks a spectator.

'Nothing each,' came the reply.

'And whit was the score at half-time?'

Ha Ha Ha!

The Gowf!

'Sandy must be the most miserable golfer I've ever had the misfortune to play with,' complained the first golfer.

'Why do you say that?' asked the second golfer.

'Well, I played golf with him last week, and after he made a hole-in-one on the fourth hole, he actually complained that he wasn't going to get the putting practice he wanted!'

Ha Ha Ha!

Two golfers were playing near the edge of their course. One of them looked over the wall in sheer amazement. 'Look, Wullie. There are two idiots fishing in that loch in this blizzard!'

Ha Ha Ha!

The old Scot was the worst player at his club in England, but challenged the club pro to a match, with a £500 bet on the side. 'But,' said the Scot, 'as you are so much better than me, jist to even things up a bit you understand, you have to let me have two "gotchies".'

The club pro hadn't a clue what a 'gotchie' was, assumed it was something Scottish, but as he was bound to win anyway, he accepted.

At the end of the game, the club members in the clubhouse were amazed to see the club pro handing over £500 to the Scot.

'For goodness sake what happened,' one member asked the pro.

'Well,' said the pro, 'I was just teeing up on the first hole, and as I swung the club, that Scotsman stuck his hand between my legs, grabbed my balls and yelled,

"Gotchie!" Have you ever played 18 holes of golf waiting for a second "gotchie"?'

Ha Ha Ha!

Two old pals were out playing a round. After one particularly long and difficult par five, one turned to the other and said, 'So how many strokes did you take at that hole?'

'Nine,' came the reply.

'Well, I took eight,' said the first. 'So that's ma hole.'

The next hole was long and quite difficult too, and after holing out, the old chap turned to his companion and asked, 'Right, how many this time?'

'Naw, naw,' replied the friend. 'it's ma turn tae ask first.'

Ha Ha Ha!

'Do you notice any improvement in me today?' asked the enthusiastic golfer of his caddie.

'Weel, sur. You've goat oan a new kilt!'

Ha Ha Ha!

'Ma doctor has advised me to give up the golf,' said the man to his friend.

'Why is that? Did he examine your heart?'

'Naw, ma score card!'

Ha Ha Ha!

'Why don't ye play with Neil anymore?' a wife asked her husband.

'Listen tae me, hen. Wid you play with somebody who deliberately coughs halfway through his opponent's back-swing, lies about his handicap and moves his ball to a better lie when he thinks nobody is looking?'

'I certainly would not!' replied the wife.

'Well, neither will Neil.'

Ha Ha Ha!

Jean and Heather ran into each other at the golf club.

'So, I hear you and Iain were recently in the Holy Land?'

'You're right. It was the worst time of my life.'

'Was there trouble in the Middle East?'

'Who said anything about the Middle East? We went to St Andrews and it didnae stop raining.'

Ha Ha Ha!

A Scotsman played with the same golf ball for over 20 years. One day the unthinkable happened. He lost the ball. He walked into the golf shop, completely disgusted.

'Well, Angus,' he announced, 'here I am again!'

Ha Ha Ha!

Two friends who hadn't seen each other for some time ran into each other at the local golf course.

'Hey, Wullie,' exclaimed Johnnie, 'you look smashing, man. Have you lost weight?'

'Aye, I've been on the golf diet noo for two months.'

'Never heard of that before. What's the golf diet?'

'It's really simple,' explained Willie. 'You give up the chips and just live on the greens.'

Ha Ha Ha!

A young Edinburgh man went for a round of golf with a girl he fancied. Beforehand, he slipped a couple of golf balls into his trouser pockets. When he met up with the girl on the first tee she couldn't help but notice the bulge in his trousers.

'It's only golf balls,' he explained.

'Oh, I'm so sorry,' she replied. 'Is that like tennis elbow?'

Ha Ha Ha!

The English

As the world climate changes and the temperatures drop …

At 40 degrees Australians shiver uncontrollably.

Men in Scotland get their shirts off and lie on the grass in a park.

At 20 degrees Californians start to wear coats, gloves and hats.

In Scotland folks put on a T-shirt – at night.

At zero degrees people in Florida shoot themselves.

In Scotland people go swimming.

At 50 degrees below zero, polar bears start to leave the Artic.

In Scotland people put on a fleece.

At 100 degrees below zero Santa Claus resigns and leaves the North Pole.

In Scotland cows complain of farmers with cold hands.

At 500 degrees below zero Hell freezes over.

People in Scotland now support England when they play Germany.

Ha Ha Ha!

An English boy and a Scottish boy were talking about who was the most intelligent.

'When I was only eight months old, I could walk,' boasted the English child.

'You think you're clever. When ah wis that age ah let them carry me!'

Ha Ha Ha!

Two Scotsmen and two Englishmen were on the Edinburgh to Glasgow train. 'By jove, it's jolly expensive on this train,' said one of the Englishmen.

'You should dae whit we dae,' replied one of the Scots. 'Both of us travel together but only buy one ticket. That way we save half the fare.'

'How so you manage that, old chap? Surely the ticket collector cómes round.'

'Easy, peasy,' said the Scotsman. 'Jist watch this.'

At the first sign of the ticket collector the two Scots went into the toilet and locked the door. When the ticket collector knocked on the door and shouted, 'Tickets please,' a single arm came round the door. The collector examined the ticket and went on.

The Englishmen were impressed and decided they would try the same trick the following day. To the Englishmen's surprise the same two Scots were on the train, but this time they hadn't bought even one ticket.

'You'll never get away with it today,' said the Englishmen.

'Well, jist you wait an' see,' replied the Scots.

When the ticket collector approached, both groups entered different toilets and locked the doors. Then one of the Scots left their toilet and knocked on the door of the toilets where the Englishmen were, shouting, 'Tickets, please.'

Ha Ha Ha!

Two Scottish scientists were discussing their research methods. 'We're no longer using rats in our experiments,' said one fellow, 'we now use Englishmen.'

'Englishmen instead of rats?' queried the other. 'What's the advantage in that?'

'Well,' said the first scientist, 'you know how it is. You get so attached to rats.'

Ha Ha Ha!

A tourist was chatting to a Scot in the Highlands.

'Do you get many English people in Scotland?'

'Aye, we do,' replied the Scot, 'but the real plague is these blasted midges!'

Ha Ha Ha!

A Scot and an Englishman lived next door to each other. The Scot owned a hen and each morning would look in the garden and pick up the hen's egg for breakfast.

One morning when he looked in the garden he saw that his hen had laid its egg in the English fellow's garden. He was about to go and get it when the Englishman came out of his house and picked up the egg. The Scot ran up to the Englishman and told him that the egg was his as it was his hen. The Englishman disagreed on the basis that the egg was laid on his property. They argued back and forth for some time before the Scot said, 'In ma clan we have a way of deciding disputes. First I kick you in the balls and we time how lang it takes you to get up. Then you kick me in the balls and we see how lang it takes me to recover. Whoever recovers quickest gets the egg.'

The Englishman agreed, so the Scot took a few steps back then ran at the Englishman kicking him heavily in the balls. The Englishman fell to the ground and rolled around in agony for 20 minutes.

Then the Englishman stood up and said, 'Right, now it's my turn to kick you in the balls.'

'Aw forget it, pal,' said the Scot, 'jist you keep the egg!'

Ha Ha Ha!

An English party at the hotel decided to join in that night's Ceilidh.

One of the Englishmen asked a young local girl up for a dance. Unfortunately the Englishman proved to be somewhat clumsy and said to the girl, 'Sorry, but I'm a little stiff from rugby.'

'Ah dinnae care where ye're fae. Jist stop standing oan ma good shoes!'

Ha Ha Ha!

A well-dressed lady walked into the foyer of a small hotel, and asked for a room for the night. 'Hey, ur you English?' asked the male receptionist.

'Yes, I am indeed.'

'Well, piss off. There is nae accommodation here fur the likes o' youse.'

'This is ridiculous!' exclaims the woman. 'Please let me speak to the manager.'

'Listen, you. Ah'm the manager and ah'm the owner.'

'Ridiculous!' she spouts and walks out.

A friend of the manager came over and asked how business was.

'Bloody terrible. If it keeps oan like this I'll need tae go back up tae Scotland!'

Ha Ha Ha!

Q. What's the difference between the Loch Ness Monster and a good Englishman?

A. The Loch Ness Monster has, on occasion, been seen.

Ha Ha Ha!

A tour bus full of tourists arrived at Culloden. 'This is where the Scots routed the English in 1746,' announced the driver.

A lady passenger replied, 'But surely the English beat the Scots?'

'No' while ah'm driving this bus, hen!'

Ha Ha Ha!

Teacher to class. 'What did the Scots call Scotland before the English arrived?'

Wee Jimmy stuck up his hand. 'Oors, sir!'

Ha Ha Ha!

A Russian, a Cuban, a Scot and an Englishman were all travelling on a train in Scotland.

The Russian, in an attempt to impress the others, said, 'In Russia we have so much Vodka we can afford to throw it away.' He then pulled out a bottle of vodka and threw it out the window. The Cuban, not to be outdone, said, 'In Cuba we have so many cigars that we can afford to throw them away.' He then pulled out a box of cigars and threw them out the window. The Scotsman, not to be outdone, said, 'In Scotland we have …' grabbed the Englishman and threw him out the window!

Ha Ha Ha!

A Scottish orchestra hired a new English conductor. He started the first rehearsal by shouting at the orchestra, 'You're a bunch of lazy Scottish twits. You don't practice enough. From now on you will get here two hours early to warm up before I grace you with my genius.'

This really annoyed the musicians, especially the percussionist, who banged at his drums – BOOM! BOOM! BOOOOM! – in protest and frustration.

The new conductor glared at the orchestra, 'Right, who did that?'

Ha Ha Ha!

The English friends of a Scot living in London were bored by his telling them how wonderful Scotland was.

'If Scotland is so bloody marvellous,' asked one, 'How come you didn't stay there?'

'The trouble is that they're all so clever up there, I had to come down here to have any chance of getting on.'

Ha Ha Ha!

On holiday the Scot was talking to a very boastful Englishman. 'So where do you come from?' asked the Scot.'

'From God's own country.'

'In that case,' replied the Scot. 'You've got the worst Scottish accent I've ever heard!'

Ha Ha Ha!

It must be acknowledged that the Scots didn't invent everything. For instance the English invented the toilet seat. It should be noted that the Scots put the hole in it.

Ha Ha Ha!

'Listen, you,' said the Englishman to the rather boastful Scot, 'take away your mountains, glens, lochs, salmon, oil and whisky and what have you got?'

'England!'

Ha Ha Ha!

Letter to an Agony Aunt in a Scottish newspaper.

'Dear Auntie Jessie,

My mother was born in Scotland and my father in England. My brother is a drug-dealer and in Barlinnie. My big sister and my wee sister are both "on-the-game" in Glasgow. I've met a wonderful man who has asked me to marry him. Should I tell him ma fether's English?'

Ha Ha Ha!

Q. Why do only one per cent of Englishmen go to Heaven?'

A. If they all went, it would be sheer hell!

Ha Ha Ha!

'How come Scotland has got all these mountains?' a tourist asked a guide.

'Over the years we have won so much land from the English we had to pile it up somewhere!'

Ha Ha Ha!

Prudence
and Money

For a birthday present a laird gave his gamekeeper a deerstalker hat with earflaps. The gamekeeper was delighted with the present and always wore it with the flaps tied under his chin to keep his ears warm.

One cold, windy day the Laird saw that the gamekeeper was not wearing the deerstalker, and asked why it was missing.

'Och, sur, I've given up wearing it since the wee accident.'

'Accident? I didn't know you had been involved in an accident.'

'Aye, sur. A man offered me a dram o' whisky but I had the earflaps doon and never heard him.'

Ha Ha Ha!

Two Scottish brothers were in business together. At the end of the financial year they attempted to balance the books but, regardless how often they tried, they were always five pounds short.

'Noo, tell me the truth, Hamish,' asked his brother. 'Are you keeping a wee wuman oan the side?'

Ha Ha Ha!

'So you're going ahead with the wedding after all, Jock?'

'Aye. She's put oan so much weight we couldn't get the engagement ring aff her finger!'

Ha Ha Ha!

It was announced recently that boards are to be placed over the bottom of the toilet doors at Aberdeen station. A spokesman said this was to prevent any limbo dancers getting in free.

Ha Ha Ha!

Old Jock and his wife lived by a loch in the Highlands. It was March, and spring had almost come. Jock asked his wife if she would walk across the frozen loch to the shop and get him a bottle of whisky. She asked for some money but he told her to put it on his slate.

When she arrived back with the whisky, she asked why he hadn't given her any money.

'I wasn't sure how thick the ice was.'

Ha Ha Ha!

The old Scotsman was on his deathbed. He looked up and asked. 'Is my wife here?'

His wife replied. 'Yes, dear, I'm here.'

'Are the weans here?'

'Yes, Paw. We're aw here.'

'Are aw the relatives here?'

'Yes, we are aw here.'

The old Scotsman got out the bed, opened the door and said. 'Well, why the hell is the light on in the hall?'

Ha Ha Ha!

A tourist in Scotland stopped in a village. Talking to one of the locals he asked if it was a healthy place to live.

'Och aye, sur. In fact there's only been one death here in the last seven years, and that was the local undertaker.'

'That's very interesting,' observed the tourist. 'And tell me, what did he die of?'

'Starvation!'

Ha Ha Ha!

The Scotsman decided to cut down on his expenditure so he gave up using aftershave. He now uses Pledge … hopes the women will take a shine to him!

Ha Ha Ha!

On their 40th wedding anniversary, Jimmy bought his wife a lair in the local cemetery. As their 41st anniversary approached, his wife asked him what he was giving her as a present this year.

'Nothing!' he replied. 'Ye still huvnae used the wan ah gave ye last year.'

Ha Ha Ha!

'Are you coming to ma house-warming party on Saturday night?' asked Jimmy.

'Wouldn't miss it fur anything, Jock. What's the address?'

'Flat number 58, Town Buildings. Jist ring the bell wi' yer elbow.'

'Can ah no' press the bell wi' ma finger, then, Jock?'

'You'll surely no' be coming empty handed?'

Ha Ha Ha!

The Scottish driving examiner asked Sandy what he would do if he was going down a very steep hill and the brakes failed.

'I'd hit something cheap.'

'You've passed!'

Ha Ha Ha!

The Englishman was in a pub when he spotted someone he thought he knew. 'Are you Jimmy McGonigal, the Scotsman?' he asked.

'Well, I'm certainly Scottish,' came the reply, 'but I'm not him.'

'Amazing,' replied the Englishman, 'you look just like him. You must have a double.'

'Thanks very much,' said the Scotsman, 'I'll have a malt.'

Ha Ha Ha!

A Scotsman went into a baker's shop. 'How much for these two cakes, please?'

'Seventy pence, sur.'

'And how much for just one?'

'That's 40 pence, sur.'

'Okay. I'll have the other one.'

Ha Ha Ha!

An Aberdonian wrote a letter to the Inland Revenue:
'Dear Sirs,
I cannae get tae sleep knowing I've cheated on ma income tax. I enclose a cheque for five hundred pounds.

P.S. If I still cannae get tae sleep I'll send ye the rest.'

Ha Ha Ha!

Two Scottish businessmen were talking. 'Business is terrible. I heard your shop burned down today.'

'Hush man!' said the second. 'It's tomorrow!'

Ha Ha Ha!

Sandy got a very expensive bottle of single malt for Christmas. His friend Dugald came round for a drink at New Year, and Sandy was forced to offer him a dram. He was reluctant to share too much of it with Dugald, so he said, 'say when,' as he slowly poured. Complete silence came from Dugald, so Sandy remarked, 'Did you hear that Big Effie had twins?'

'When?' said Dugald.

'Okay,' said Sandy, and put down the bottle.

Ha Ha Ha!

A guy walked into a pub in Scotland and ordered a pint of beer.

The barman pulled the pint, then said, 'That'll be 20 pence, sir.'

'Are you sure it's just 20 pence? That seems incredible,' said the guy.

'Och, there's no mistake, sur. Ma beer has been the same price since the 70s.'

The chap sipped his beer and looked across the pub at a crowd of locals playing darts. He noticed that none of them were drinking.

'Why aren't these guys drinking?' he asked the barman.

'Och,' said the barman, 'they're aw waitin' fur happy hour!'

Ha Ha Ha!

A Scot got on a London bus and put his suitcase under the stairs.

'Charing Cross, please,' said the Scot to the driver.

'That'll be £2.50 for yourself and 50 pence for your luggage.'

'Whit! I'm no' paying 50 pence for a suitcase.'

'In that case,' said the driver, 'I'm throwing it off the bus.'

This he did, but as the bus was on Westminster Bridge the suitcase fell into the River Thames.

The Scot was furious. He shouted. 'Ya dirty English crook! You're no' satisfied with trying to rob me, you're also trying to drown ma wee boy!'

Ha Ha Ha!

Did you hear the story about the lecherous old Scottish artist who lured a young lady to his flat to see his etchings.

He sold her three of them!

Ha Ha Ha!

A Scotsman was dragged before the court in Aberdeen for making nuisance phone calls. He was caught because he always reversed the charges!

Ha Ha Ha!

Old Hughie was asked why he ate nothing but baked beans on a Saturday.

'Och, that's easy. It's so I can get myself a bubble bath on a Sunday.'

Ha Ha Ha!

'Is Jamie in?' asked the caller to the small croft.

'Aye, he's in.'

'Well, can ah see him?'

'No, ye cannae see him.'

'It's jist aboot a wee bit business.'

'Sorry, but he's deed.'

'Was it awfa sudden?'

'Aye, awfa sudden.'

'Weel, did he say anything aboot a pot o' red paint afore he passed away?'

Ha Ha Ha!

Ramblers from Aberdeen were caught in a dreadful snowstorm up in the Cairngorms, but they managed to take refuge in a bothy.

A couple of days later a search party knocked at the snow-bound hut.

'Wha's there?' came a voice from within.

'It's the Red Cross.'

'We gave last year,' was the reply.

Ha Ha Ha!

Wee MacAferty went to the barbers in Stirling.

'Hoo much fur a haircut?'

'Four pounds 50 pence.'

'Well, whit dae ye charge fur a shave then?'

'Two pounds.'

'OK. Jist shave ma heid!'

Ha Ha Ha!

Aberdonians have a great cure for sea-sickness. They lean over the side of the ship with a 50 pence coin in their teeth.

Ha Ha Ha!

Gerry's wife was not so good with the money, so he determined to have a wee discussion with her about the economics of life.

The following day his pal asked how he he had got on with the chat to his wife, and whether she got the message.

'Aye, sort of,' came Gerry's cautious reply, 'I'm going to have to give up whisky and fags!'

Ha Ha Ha!

Old Hamish was giving instructions to his eldest son regarding his funeral arrangements. 'No, son, make sure you go roon the entire company and ensure that they all have a dram of whisky. Then, after a while, you go roon again and make sure they all have another dram. An' since ah'll no' be there, ah'll jist hae a couple o' drams right noo.'

Ha Ha Ha!

Scotty had just read that the richest man in Scotland had died. Suddenly he burst into floods of tears before being comforted by his pal, Willie.

'Come on, Scotty,' said Willie, 'pull yourself together man. Why, ye didnae even know the fellow.'

'Ah know. That's why ah'm crying!'

Ha Ha Ha!

Sandy had been out for the evening with his girlfriend. When he got home his father was sitting up waiting for him. 'Have you been oot wi' that lassie again?' he demanded.

'Ah was, Dad,' replied the son, 'but why are you so worried looking?'

'I wis jist wondering what the evening cost?'

'Well, no more than two pounds, Dad.'

'Okay, that wisna too bad, son.'

'It wis aw she had on her, Dad.'

Ha Ha Ha!

A loud voice was heard in a bank in Aberdeen. 'Did anybody drap a roll of notes wi' a rubber band roon them?'

'Aye, ah did!' said various voices.

'Well, ah jist found the rubber band!'

Ha Ha Ha!

'I'm afraid you are going to need a lot of private medical treatment,' said the specialist to McDuff. 'It will probably cost you a thousand pounds.'

'A thousand pounds! Doctor, I'm not a wealthy man.'

'Ok. In that case I'll make it five hundred pounds.'

'Doctor, you've got to understand. I have five children to support plus my old father who lives with us.'

'All right. For you I'll make it two hundred pounds. But tell me this, why did you come to my private clinic? I'm the most expensive specialist in Edinburgh.'

'When in comes to my health, doctor,' replied McDuff, 'money is no object!'

Ha Ha Ha!

For Sale: Used gravestone. Ideal for family called MacDonald.

Ha Ha Ha!

The Insurance Agent received a frantic call from a Scotsman.

'Ah want tae insure ma hoose. Can ah do it noo over the phone?'

'Sorry, sur,' said the Insurance Agent, 'but I have to see it first.'

'Well, ye had better get a move on, the place is on fire!'

Ha Ha Ha!

'Can I interest you in a nice pocket calculator, sur?' asked the shop assistant.

'No, thanks,' said Wullie, 'ah already know how many pockets ah have.'

Ha Ha Ha!

After a rather poor collection was gathered in, the minister prayed, 'We thank you, dear Lord, that the plate has been returned safely.'

Ha Ha Ha!

Jock decided to be bold and bought two tickets for a raffle. One of his tickets won him a hundred pounds. When asked how he felt about his win he replied. 'I'm fair annoyed. Ma other ticket didnae win anything.'

Ha Ha Ha!

Wee McGregor went into the fish and chip shop. 'Twenty pence worth o' chips, please. I want three pence worth o' pickled onions and ah want loads and loads o' salt and vinegar on the lot. Oh, and by the way, could you wrap them in today's *Daily Record*?'

Ha Ha Ha!

Willie understood money but his wife, Heather, still had some way to go. One day he said to her, 'Listen, Pet, you know that cheque you wrote last month. Well, the bank have returned it.'
'Smashing! What will I spend it on next?'

Ha Ha Ha!

Q. What's the difference between a Scotsman and a canoe?
A. A canoe will sometimes tip!

Ha Ha Ha!

An Aberdonian was ill with mumps. 'Send fur ma creditors,' he said, 'At last I can give them something!'

Ha Ha Ha!

'Hey, Gordon, I hear you are a great believer in free speech.'

'I am that, Jock.'

'Great, can ah use yer mobile!'

Ha Ha Ha!

A Scot died and went to heaven. 'You have been a bad man during your life,' said Saint Peter. 'You cannot come in unless you pass a test. Take this old bucket and go and empty the Clyde.'

'But the Clyde is filled with water from the Atlantic. That's an unfair thing to ask. Is there no alternative?'

'Well,' replied Saint Peter, 'you could go to the Fisherman's Rest Pub in Aberdeen, and stand beside one of the regulars until they buy you a whisky.'

'Gies that auld bucket!'

Ha Ha Ha!

Two old cons were talking in Barlinnie Jail in Glasgow. 'You might not believe this, Pat, but I used to live the life of Riley. I had a villa in Tuscany, a Mercedes and a Jaguar, plenty of women, and I ate in nothing but the very best of restaurants.'

'So, what happened?' asked the other prisoner.

'Riley reported that his credit cards were missing!'

Ha Ha Ha!

'My heavens,' exclaimed McCulloch's friend, 'you seem tae have lost yer stutter?'

'Aye,' replied McCulloch, 'ye see I've had to phone Australia a lot!'

Ha Ha Ha!

A chap was in a restaurant in Aberdeen reading the menu. When the waitress came over he asked, 'Why do twa boiled eggs cost twice as much as a three egg omelette?'

'Och,' said the waitress, 'it's because ye cannae count the eggs in an omelette.'

Ha Ha Ha!

Scottish History

At an archaeological dig in Stirling the skeleton of a man was found. The professor who examined the remains announced. 'This skeleton was of a happy man who died almost seven hundred years ago.'

'That's amazing, professor,' said a journalist, 'but how can you tell?'

'Easy. He had a piece of paper in his hand that said, "Five shillings on Robert the Bruce"!'

Ha Ha Ha!

The guide showing tourists around Stirling Castle pointed to a skull and said, 'Ladies and gentlemen. Here is the skull of Braveheart himself, William Wallace.'

'But surely that is the skull of a boy?' questioned one of the party.

'It is indeed, sur. That was when he wis jist a lad!'

Ha Ha Ha!

The historian visiting Edinburgh Castle was keen to find the last resting place of Bonnie Prince Charlie. So he asked his guide if he could help him.

'Certainly, sur. I know the very spot. However I would expect such valuable information would be worth a little something.' A large note was duly slipped into the guide's hand.

'You're very lucky, sur,' explained the guide. 'For the Prince himself is buried inside this very bit of the wall of the Castle.'

'That's amazing!' exclaimed the historian. 'But are you absolutely sure?'

'Of course I am, sur. Have you never heard of the auld song, *Bonnie Charlie's noo awa*.'

Ha Ha Ha!

'Aye, ma great-grandfather shot 50 Redcoats wi the wan bullet.'

'Amazing! How did he manage that?'

'They were coming up the glen in single file!'

Ha Ha Ha!

For centuries, Berwick-on-Tweed, right on the border between Scotland and England, was either Scottish or English, depending on the outcome of various battles fought there between the countries.

Eventually, it was settled that Berwick-on-Tweed was English. When the Mayor of the town was asked how he felt now it was finally established that the town was English, he said, 'Thank heavens, I couldn't have stood another Scottish winter!'

Ha Ha Ha!

Scottish
Health
Service

'I am not saying that the Health Service is bad, but one or two hospitals still send patients to Glasgow airport for x-rays.'

Ha Ha Ha!

A Bearsden man went to the doctor. 'Doctor, doctor, I keep thinking I'm a bottle of gin.'

'You probably need some more tonic.'

Ha Ha Ha!

The family GP pulled the sheet up over the patient's face and turned to the anxious wife.

'First the good news, Mrs MacDonald. His temperature has gone down.'

Ha Ha Ha!

A highly excited man rang up the Scottish ambulance service. 'Quick, quick, come quick,' he shouted, 'ma wife's havin' a baby!'

'Is this her first child?' asked the operator.

'Naw, ya twit, this is her husband!'

Ha Ha Ha!

'What's wrong, doctor? You look puzzled.'

'I don't know exactly what is wrong with you, but I think it's the result of drinking too much whisky.'

'Don't worry, doctor. I'll just come back when you're sober.'

Ha Ha Ha!

A lady goes to the doctors in Airdrie and says, 'Doctor, ma husband limps because his right leg is three inches shorter than his left leg. Whit wid you do in his case?'

'Probably limp as well!'

Ha Ha Ha!

A very heavy drinker was warned by his doctor that if he didn't reduce his consumption of alcohol he would be dead in a couple of years. 'You have got to cut down to three drinks each day,' said the doctor. The drinker agreed and left. A few weeks later the doctor met the chap in the street. The guy was the worse for wear.

'Hey,' said the doctor, 'I thought you agreed to three drinks a day?'

'Yer right, doc,' said the drunk, 'but ah went tae another four doctors for second opinions and they prescribed the same!'

Ha Ha Ha!

The doctor was chatting to his new patient. 'I'm afraid your records haven't reached us yet from your previous doctor, and as my scales are broken at present perhaps you could tell me your average weight.'

'Sorry, doctor,' replied the patient, 'ah dinnae ken.'

'Well, do you know the heaviest weight you have ever been?'

'Ah think it wis 12 stone nine pounds, doctor,' replied the patient.

'And what is the least you have weighed?'

'Ah think it was six and a half pounds.'

Ha Ha Ha!

Three different Scotsmen were posed the question, 'If you were told by your doctor that you only had three months to live, what would you do?'

The first man replied, 'Well, I would settle my affairs, live a quiet contemplative life, attend the church and prepare for the end.'

The second man said, 'I would go on a luxury cruise, then blow all my money on a farewell booze-up.'

The third man said, 'Ah wid get a second opinion!'

Ha Ha Ha!

A Scottish doctor and his wife were having an argument before he went off to his surgery. 'And, another thing,' he screamed as he went out the door, 'you're no bloody good in bed either!'

By late afternoon he had cooled down and decided to call his wife. After many rings the phone was eventually picked up. 'What took you so long to answer?' he asked.

'I was in bed.'

'In bed, at this time of the day?' he queried.

'Just getting a second opinion, dear!'

Ha Ha Ha!

In the middle of the night, Susan awoke with a terrible pain. 'Quick, quick,' she screamed at her husband, Willie. 'Get the doctor. Ah think it's ma appendix.'

Willie immediately phoned the doctor. 'Doctor, it's my wife. She's screaming with terrible pain. She thinks it's her appendix.'

'Listen, Willie,' said the doctor, 'calm down, man. Remember I took out yer wife's appendix in an emergency operation about five years ago. In all ma time as a doctor, I've never heard of anyone having another one.'

'That may be so,' replied Willie, 'but have ye never heard of anyone having another wife?'

Ha Ha Ha!

'Oh, doctor,' said Maggie, 'Ah'm awfa afraid ah'm gonnae die.'

'Dinnae worry, Maggie,' replied the doctor, 'that's the last thing you're going to dae.'

Ha Ha Ha!

The doctor examined Sandy and informed him that he was incontinent.

'Don't be silly, doctor,' he protested, 'ah've never been oot o' Scotland!'

Ha Ha Ha!

'My doctor has put me on a new diet. I've to use only vegetable and corn oil when making the haggis,' said one lady to another.

'And is it working?'

'Sort of. I haven't lost any weight but ma voice no longer squeaks.'

Ha Ha Ha!

The doctor didn't stay long at the croft. 'Och, he's fine. He's a hypochondriac and just thinks he's sick.'

A couple of days later the doctor once more appeared at the croft door. 'I wis just passing,' said the doctor, 'an' I thought I would just check up how yer husband is.'

'Och, he's much worse today, doctor,' said the lady. 'Noo he thinks he's deed!'

Ha Ha Ha!

Old Peter had a serious hearing problem and finally got fitted with a small NHS hearing aid. A few months later he met a friend in the street, who remarked, 'your family must be very glad you can hear again.'

'Och,' replied the old man, 'I haven't told them yet. So far I've changed ma will four times!'

Ha Ha Ha!

The Aberdonian patient asked his dentist, 'Would you kindly tell me how much you charge to have this tooth extracted?'

'Forty-five pounds,' replied the dentist.

'Forty-five pounds for just a few minutes work?' queried the patient.

'Well, I can do it much slower if you like.'

Ha Ha Ha!

The doctor phoned his patient and said, 'I've got some good news and some bad news for you, Hamish.'

'What's the good news, doctor?'

'They're going to name a disease after you!'

Ha Ha Ha!

The old lady in Paisley went to see the doctor, complaining of a pain in her left foot.

'Och,' said the doctor, 'it'll jist be old age.'

'It cannae be that,' replied the woman, 'the ither yin is fine and it's the same age!'

Ha Ha Ha!

Ha Ha Ha! Ha Ha Ha! Ha Ha Ha! Ha Ha Ha!

Ha Ha Ha! Ha Ha Ha!

The Naughty Ones!

A Scottish publishing mogul was asked what the difference was between English and Scottish magazines.

'That's easy. If you buy *Cosmopolitan* it tells you how to have an orgasm. If you buy *The People's Friend* it tells you how to knit one!'

Ha Ha Ha!

Mr Grouse came back to the nest and saw that one of the eggs was completely different from the rest. 'How come this egg is different?' he asked Mrs Grouse.

'Och,' she replied. 'I just did it for a lark!'

Ha Ha Ha!

Two Edinburgh friends in their 60s had both lost their partners and decided to get married. One night over dinner they ran through the various details of their forthcoming arrangements. 'What are we going to do with both houses?' asked the woman.

'I think,' says the man, 'we ought to sell our homes, and then we can both pay half of the cost of a new home. Now, dear, how would you like to go about the shopping bills?'

'Well,' observed the woman, 'we are not big eaters so why don't we just split the bill in half. And it's probably best doing the same with the electricity, gas, Council Tax and all these kinds of things.'

'Good idea,' says the man. 'Now one final thing. What about sex?'

'Preferably infrequently, dearest,' replies the woman.

'Excuse me, darling, but was that one word or two?'

Ha Ha Ha!

A couple were celebrating their 40th wedding anniversary with a slap-up meal.

The wife turned to the man and said, 'You know, darling, I still love when we have sex together.'

The husband thought about this for a couple of minutes then said, 'So do I, dear, but I think on balance I prefer Hogmanay.'

The wife was taken aback. 'Don't you prefer sex?'

'Difficult to say,' he replied. 'it's just that Hogmanay comes round more often!'

Ha Ha Ha!

A Wee Mixture

Two Scots were fishing on the River Tay. After the fishing finished for the day they started to swap stories. The first fisherman told of a tremendous struggle he had once had with a 300 lb salmon. The second fisherman listened quietly, and then admitted he had never caught anything quite so big.

However, he told the first fisherman of a time when his hook snagged a lantern from the depths. When he examined the lantern he discovered it was very old, but the strange thing was that the candle was still lit.

For a long time both Scots sat in silence. Finally the first one took a long draw on his pipe and said, 'Listen, McTavish. I'll take 150 lbs aff ma salmon if you'll pit the light oot in yer lantern!'

Ha Ha Ha!

A Scottish marriage is a solemn and dignified affair.

In the first year the man speaks and the woman listens. In the second year the woman speaks and the man listens. In the third year they both speak … and the neighbours listen!

Ha Ha Ha!

A man walks into a pub in Dundee and the barman says, 'Whit'll ye be having, sur?'

'Got any electric soup?' asks the man.

'Naw,' replies the barman, 'we only sell beer, lager and whisky.'

'Okay,' says the man, and he leaves.

The same man comes into the bar the next day and says to the same barman, 'Got any electric soup?'

'Naw,' replies the barman, 'we only sell beer, lager and whisky.'

'Okay,' says the man, and he leaves.

The day after that the same man comes into the bar and says to the same barman, 'Got any electric soup?'

'Listen, you,' says the barman, 'Ah told you yesterday we don't sell electric soup. If you come in this pub again I'm going to nail you to this bar!' So, the man leaves.

The next day the man enters the pub again and says to the same barman, 'Got any nails?'

'Naw, why?' asked the barman.

'In that case, got any electric soup?'

Ha Ha Ha!

A man walked into a bar in Edinburgh and sat down next to a man with a dog at his feet. 'Does yer dog bite?' he asked.

'Naw, ma dog doesna bite,' came the reply.

So he reached down to give the dog a pat, and the dog bit him.

'Hey, whit's the game here?' exclaimed the man. 'Ah thought you said your dug doesna bite?'

'Aye, ah did. But that's no' ma dug!'

Ha Ha Ha!

A Scottish pig walked into a pub, ordered 20 whiskies and drank the lot.

'Wid ye like to know where the gents is?' asked the barman.

'Naw, naw, ah'm the wee pig that goes wee, wee, wee all the way home!'

Ha Ha Ha!

Three whisky magnates had a meeting in a hotel bar.

'Okay, barman,' said the first one, 'give me a Japanese whisky, the finest whisky in the world.' The barman gives him his drink.

'Right, barman,' said the second magnate, 'give me an American whiskey, the finest whiskey in the world.' The barman gives him his drink.

'Right, barman,' says the Scottish magnate, 'give me a Coke.'

The two other magnates were astonished and asked, 'Why aren't you drinking Scotch?'

'Well,' says the Scot, 'I reckoned if you guys aren't drinking whisky, neither would I.'

Ha Ha Ha!

Three Scottish mice walk into a pub. The Edinburgh mouse ordered a single whisky and said, 'When ah see a mousetrap, ah lie on ma back and set it off aff wi' ma foot. When the trap comes over ah catch it wi ma teeth, do 30 bench-presses, and then make aff wi the cheese.'

The Inverness mouse ordered a double whisky and said, 'When ah see rat poison, ah collect as much as ah can, take it home, and add it to ma cornflakes every morning instead o' milk.'

The Glasgow mouse said, 'Sorry, but ah cannae stay long. Ah've goat a date wi' a cat!'

Ha Ha Ha!

'Be very careful,' said the Ben Nevis guide, 'not to fall. It really is a fearsome drop. But if you do fall, remember to look over to the left. You get a wonderful view of the other mountains on that side.'

Ha Ha Ha!

Old Farmer McGinty bought a new bull. Unfortunately, despite being in a field with some young heifers, he did not seem to have an appetite for that which he had been bought. So Old Farmer McGinty called in the vet who duly prescribed some pills.

Some time later, Farmer McGinty was talking to his neighbour, Farmer McDougall. 'So how's that new bull o' yours doing noo the vet has been tae see him?'

'Man, whit a difference,' said Old Farmer McGinty. 'He's had his way with the whole herd. In fact I've given him oot on loan to Farmer McTaggart and I hear he's fairly doing the business with his coos.'

'So, whit wis the stuff that the vet gave yer bull?' asked Farmer McDougall.

'Och, it wis big, pink pills,' replied Farmer McGinty.

'An' whit kind o' pills be they?' asked Farmer McDougall.

'Och, ah dinnae ken, but they taste like strawberries!'

Ha Ha Ha!

'And how did your week's holiday in Skye go?' asked one Glaswegian of another.

'Well, it only rained twice,' came the reply.

'Twice, that was good.'

'Aye, once for three days and once for four days!'

Ha Ha Ha!

Willie was all set for his first Continental motoring holiday. Then just a couple of days before he was due to set off he cancelled the whole thing. 'Why did ye cancel yon holiday, Willie?' asked his pal. 'Wis it the language thing?'

'Naw, naw,' replied Willie, 'ah'm no' risking ma life oan they roads over there driving on the other side o' the road. Ah tried it twa days back an' it wid frighten the life oot o' ye!'

Ha Ha Ha!

The young Edinburgh chap bought a sports car, and decided to find out how it handled on quiet Highland roads. Coming across a long straight he put his foot down. The car was almost at a hundred when the road suddenly rose over a hilltop. Standing on the road was a broken down tractor, with two farm hands examining the engine. The car swerved and flew to the right, over a fence, shuddering to a halt in a ploughed field.

One farm hand said to the other, 'It's a good job we got the tractor out the field before it broke down.'

Ha Ha Ha!

Two Scottish astronauts landed on the moon. Being Scots, one immediately left the spacecraft to find a pub. When he returned his companion asked, 'Any luck, pal? Wis there a pub wi whisky?'

'Aye, but the pub wis gey poor. Nae atmosphere!'

Ha Ha Ha!